AI and Us: Navigating the Future of Work, Creativity, and Ethics"

Table of Contents for "AI and Us: Navigating the Future of Work, Creativity, and Ethics"

Chapter 1: A Glimpse into the Future

The city hummed with quiet efficiency. Cars without drivers slid through intersections in perfect synchrony, their electric engines purring softly. Drones buzzed overhead, delivering packages with the precision of a surgeon's scalpel, while pedestrians, heads down, moved briskly, engrossed in their augmented reality glasses. It was a world that seemed polished and seamless on the surface—until you noticed the quiet despair etched into the faces of those who no longer had a place in it.

Alex, a 39-year-old project manager, sat at his kitchen table, his hands gripping a cup of coffee that had gone cold. He stared blankly at the screen of his AI assistant, which had just delivered the news he feared most: his role was being automated. After 12 years of steady work in corporate project management, he was deemed redundant. His inbox contained a brief, impersonal email from HR:

Dear Alex,

We regret to inform you that your role has been automated as part of our company's ongoing commitment to innovation. We thank you for your service and encourage you to explore reskilling opportunities.

The words *reskilling opportunities* burned in his mind. What skills could he possibly learn that an AI couldn't master faster? No warning. No chance to adapt. Just a click of a button, and his livelihood was gone

Memories of Stability

Alex's apartment was a modest but comfortable space in the city's outskirts. He had worked hard to secure it—a product of late nights, tight deadlines, and an unwavering belief that hard work would always pay off. As he looked around the room, every object seemed to mock him. The leather couch he had saved for months to buy, the smart home hub that now felt more like a symbol of betrayal, and the framed photo of his daughter beaming on her fifth birthday.

His daughter, Mia, was only eight now, but she had started asking questions that made him uneasy. "Daddy, why do you work so much?" she once asked, tilting her head with innocent curiosity. "Because I want to make sure you have everything you need," he had replied. But now, as he stared at the termination email, he wondered how he could possibly keep that promise

The Streets of Protest

The corporate district was an architectural marvel, with its glass skyscrapers and automated walkways. It was also the heart of the city's growing unrest. A massive crowd had gathered in front of one of the tallest towers, its reflective surface towering like a monolith over the people it had displaced.

"Fair wages for human work!" someone shouted, their voice hoarse but defiant.

"Bring back real jobs!" echoed another, holding a sign with the words *Humans Deserve Better* scrawled in bold letters.

The air was charged with frustration and desperation. The crowd was a mix of former employees, gig workers, and students—all grappling with the same bleak reality: their skills were no longer valued in a world run by algorithms.

Alex hesitated at the edge of the crowd. He wasn't the type to protest. He had always believed in adapting, in staying ahead of the curve. But as he looked around, he saw his own fears reflected in the eyes of the people around him. A young woman in a delivery uniform clutched a sign that read,

Replaced by a Drone. An older man in a suit muttered under his breath, "Forty years of experience… gone overnight."

How We Got Here

The speakers on stage took turns addressing the crowd, each telling a story of how AI had reshaped their industries—and their lives. A teacher spoke of virtual classrooms where AI instructors tailored lessons to individual students, rendering human teachers nearly obsolete. A journalist described how algorithms could churn out articles in seconds, leaving little room for creativity or investigative reporting.

Alex listened, the stories weaving together a tapestry of loss and uncertainty. It wasn't that people hadn't seen the changes coming. The signs had been there for years—factories with robotic arms, supermarkets with self-checkout lanes, customer service lines answered by AI chatbots. But no one had anticipated the speed at which it would happen.

The Human Cost

For every innovation, there was a cost, and that cost was now glaringly apparent. Entire families were being uprooted. Communities that once thrived on local industries were now ghost towns. And while some people adapted—transitioning into tech roles or finding niche markets untouched by AI—others, like Alex, were left stranded.

The government had made promises, of course. Universal basic income, reskilling programs, and regulations to ensure ethical AI use were all touted as solutions. But these measures were either underfunded, poorly implemented, or stuck in bureaucratic limbo.

Alex's own experience with "reskilling opportunities" had been disheartening. The courses were either too generic to be useful or so advanced that they felt impossible to grasp without prior expertise. It wasn't just about learning new skills—it was about the overwhelming pace at which the world was changing.

The Bigger Picture

As Alex stood in the crowd, a thought struck him: this wasn't just about jobs. It was about humanity itself. What did it mean to live in a world where human labor was no longer needed? Where creativity and effort were overshadowed by efficiency and profit?

The questions came in waves:

• *When did convenience become more important than humanity?*

• *What happens to society when millions of people are left behind?*

• *Is there a way to coexist with AI, or are we destined to compete with it?*

Above him, the corporate tower loomed, its polished exterior reflecting the sunlight. Somewhere inside, decisions were being made—decisions about jobs, livelihoods, and the future of work. Alex couldn't help but wonder: were those decisions being made by humans or algorithms?

The protest's energy shifted as a speaker took the stage, their voice cutting through the noise. "We didn't create AI to destroy ourselves," they said. "But if we don't act now, that's exactly what will happen."

Alex found himself nodding, a flicker of determination igniting within him. The road ahead was uncertain, but one thing was clear: humanity needed a plan, or it risked losing itself entirely.

Chapter 2: The Evolution of Intelligence

Opening Scene: The Dawn of AI

It started innocently, as all revolutions do. In the mid-20th century, computers were little more than number-crunching machines. They were tools—nothing more. Yet, in the quiet halls of academia and the ambitious labs of technology pioneers, whispers of something greater began to emerge. Could machines, they wondered, not only process information but *learn* from it?

The journey of artificial intelligence began here, with a question as simple as it was profound: *What if machines could think?*

In 1956, at a small workshop in Dartmouth College, the term "artificial intelligence" was coined. It was the birth of an idea that would shape the world in ways no one could have predicted. The early years were clumsy, filled with lofty promises and limited success. Yet, from those humble beginnings, AI took its first steps toward becoming what it is today.

The First Wave: From Logic to Learning

The 1960s and 1970s marked AI's infancy, a time of experimentation and boundless optimism. Machines learned to play simple games like chess, solve basic puzzles, and even perform rudimentary translations. Programs like ELIZA, an early chatbot, mimicked human conversation, sparking excitement—and a hint of fear—about the potential of these systems.

But there were limits. Computers could follow rules, but they couldn't *understand*. The world was too complex for static algorithms, and by the 1980s, the AI field hit what became known as the "AI Winter"—a period of disillusionment and dwindling funding.

The Breakthroughs That Changed Everything

The tide turned in the 1990s and early 2000s, thanks to advances in computing power and the explosion of data. Suddenly, machines weren't just following instructions; they were learning patterns. Enter machine learning—a technology that allowed computers to improve their performance with experience.

Key milestones followed:

- In 1997, IBM's Deep Blue defeated world chess champion Garry Kasparov.

- In 2011, IBM's Watson outperformed human contestants on *Jeopardy!*

- By the mid-2010s, systems like AlphaGo demonstrated AI's ability to master games once thought impossible for machines.

Behind the scenes, neural networks—the backbone of today's AI—were evolving. Inspired by the structure of the human brain, these systems allowed machines to process vast amounts of data and make decisions with uncanny accuracy. The advent of deep learning turbocharged progress, and AI went from theoretical to practical almost overnight.

AI Enters Everyday Life

By the 2020s, AI had infiltrated nearly every industry. Virtual assistants like Siri and Alexa became household names. Netflix knew what you wanted to watch before you did. Social media platforms curated feeds that captured attention with surgical precision, shaping opinions, and behaviors in the process.

AI wasn't just a tool anymore—it was a presence, embedded in our lives. It learned from our data, predicted our desires, and even influenced our decisions. The world was becoming smarter, faster, and more connected. But with every advancement came questions about control, ethics, and the human cost of progress.

The Dual Nature of Innovation

While some celebrated AI as the greatest technological breakthrough since the internet, others warned of its darker side. Automation was a double-edged sword. It improved efficiency, yes, but at what cost? As industries embraced AI, millions of workers found themselves displaced. Factories became fully automated, customer service went virtual, and entire job categories vanished.

For every life made easier by AI, there was another left in chaos. The global economy shifted, creating winners and losers. Nations that invested heavily in AI research and infrastructure thrived, while others fell behind, deepening global inequalities.

The Quiet Revolution

The most profound impact of AI wasn't the flashy technology we saw—it was the silent changes happening beneath the surface. Algorithms decided who got loans, who was hired, and even who was granted bail. AI systems influenced elections, manipulated markets, and redefined power structures.

And yet, for most people, these changes felt invisible. The world kept spinning, seemingly as it always had. But Alex, like many others, began to see the cracks. The systems that promised efficiency and fairness often perpetuated biases, favoring those who already held power.

Chapter 3: The Allure of Automation

In a sprawling warehouse on the outskirts of Shenzhen, rows of robotic arms moved in synchronized harmony. With laser precision, they assembled smartphones, performing tasks once handled by hundreds of workers. The scene was mesmerizing: efficient, tireless, and flawless. Automation wasn't just a technological achievement—it was an economic revolution.

The CEO of the company overseeing the operation spoke proudly during a press conference:

"This is the future of productivity. Faster production, lower costs, and zero human error."

Investors cheered. Governments touted the innovation as a model for progress. But far from the camera's glare, the human cost of this revolution began to grow.

Automation promised a golden era for businesses and governments alike. The appeal was irresistible:

1. Cost Savings: Machines didn't need salaries, benefits, or breaks. Once the initial investment was made, they became the cheapest workforce imaginable.

2. Efficiency: Unlike humans, machines didn't tire or make mistakes. They could work 24/7, ensuring faster production and consistent quality.

3. Scalability: Automation allowed companies to meet growing demand without the challenges of hiring and training more staff.

For CEOs, these benefits translated into higher profits, satisfied shareholders, and a competitive edge in a cutthroat global market.

Governments also saw potential. Automation could bolster GDP, reduce reliance on foreign labor, and position nations as leaders in the global economy. For a time, the benefits seemed undeniable.

But automation wasn't just about improving efficiency—it was about replacing humans. Entire industries were transformed:

- Manufacturing: Once the backbone of middle-class employment, factories became dominated by robotic systems. Assembly line jobs disappeared almost overnight.

- Retail: Self-checkout kiosks replaced cashiers, and warehouses shifted to fully automated systems, reducing the need for human staff.

- Transportation: Autonomous trucks and taxis began to edge out drivers, threatening one of the largest employment sectors globally.

- Customer Service: Chatbots and AI-driven call centers became the norm, rendering thousands of support agents obsolete.

The losses were staggering. By the late 2020s, studies showed that nearly 40% of jobs worldwide were at risk of being automated. The trend wasn't limited to low-skill roles. Even professions like law, medicine, and finance faced disruption as AI systems became capable of performing tasks once reserved for highly educated specialists.

One of automation's less obvious appeals was its ability to leverage data. Algorithms could process vast amounts of information, identifying patterns and trends that human minds couldn't grasp. Businesses used this capability to:

- Optimize supply chains.

- Predict consumer behavior.

- Customize marketing campaigns.

For companies, data-driven decision-making meant reduced waste, increased profits, and more personalized customer experiences. But for workers like Alex, it meant something more troubling: decisions that once involved human judgment were now dictated by cold, impersonal algorithms.

For all its benefits, automation brought unintended consequences.

- Job Losses: Millions of people were displaced, struggling to find new roles in an increasingly automated world.

- Economic Inequality: While companies profited, wealth became concentrated in the hands of a few, leaving vast portions of the population behind.

- Over-Reliance on Technology: Businesses that embraced automation too quickly found themselves vulnerable. When systems failed or were hacked, entire operations ground to a halt.

The societal impact was profound. Communities built around industries like manufacturing and transportation crumbled. Families who had relied on stable, middle-class jobs found themselves trapped in cycles of poverty.

For Alex, the allure of automation had once seemed distant—something that affected factories in faraway countries. But now, it was personal. The project management software that had replaced him could analyze data faster, produce reports instantly, and even suggest solutions to problems.

"How do you compete with perfection?" Alex muttered one evening, staring at his computer screen. It wasn't just about losing his job—it was about losing the sense of purpose that came with it.

Chapter 4: When Machines Learn

It was 2 a.m., and the laboratory was quiet except for the soft hum of servers and the occasional click of a keyboard. Dr. Rachel Kim, a leading AI researcher, leaned back in her chair, watching a monitor display a cascade of numbers and patterns. The AI system she had spent months training was solving a problem she hadn't explicitly programmed it to tackle. It wasn't just following instructions—it was learning.

For the first time, Rachel felt both exhilaration and unease. *This machine*, she thought, *is thinking in ways I don't fully understand.*

AI took its most significant leap forward when it transitioned from rule-based systems to machine learning. Instead of relying on pre-written instructions, these systems were designed to learn patterns and make decisions based on data.

Key to this evolution was the development of algorithms that could:

> 1. Recognize Patterns: From images to text, these systems could identify subtle trends in data.
>
> 2. Adapt Over Time: As more data was fed into the system, it improved its performance without human intervention.
>
> 3. Make Predictions: By analyzing historical data, machine learning systems could anticipate future outcomes with remarkable accuracy.

One of the most transformative breakthroughs was the development of neural networks—algorithms inspired by the structure of the human brain. These networks enabled machines to process information in layers, uncovering complex relationships that humans might miss.

Deep learning, a subset of machine learning, revolutionized AI by enabling machines to perform tasks previously thought impossible. This technology powered:

- Image Recognition: AI systems that could identify faces, objects, and even emotions in photos and videos.

- Natural Language Processing (NLP): Tools like virtual assistants and chatbots capable of understanding and generating human-like language.

- Autonomous Systems: Self-driving cars and drones that could navigate the world with minimal human input.

Deep learning relied on massive datasets and powerful GPUs (graphic processing units) to process information. The more data the system had, the smarter it became.

But this reliance on data came with a cost:

- Biases in Data: AI systems often inherited the biases of the data they were trained on, leading to ethical dilemmas.

- Privacy Concerns: The vast amounts of personal data required for training raised questions about surveillance and consent.

Big data was the fuel that powered modern AI. Every search query, social media post, and online purchase added to the ocean of information that AI systems analyzed. Companies like Google, Amazon, and Facebook built empires by collecting and leveraging this data, creating AI tools that were both incredibly powerful and deeply invasive.

Alex remembered the first time he'd noticed just how much data companies were collecting. He had searched online for a new bike, and for weeks afterward, every website he visited was filled with ads for cycling gear. At first, it seemed convenient. But over time, it felt unsettling—like the AI systems knew more about him than he knew about himself. The most significant leap came when AI systems began making decisions without human oversight. These systems could:

- Optimize Supply Chains: Adjusting logistics in real-time to meet demand.

- Trade Stocks: Making split-second decisions in financial markets.

- Diagnose Diseases: Analyzing medical images with accuracy that rivaled human doctors.

But with this autonomy came risks. In 2016, an autonomous AI system in the stock market caused a flash crash, wiping out billions of dollars in value within minutes. The event highlighted a critical issue: when machines act independently, who is accountable for their actions?

One of the most troubling aspects of modern AI was the "black box problem." Even the engineers who built these systems often couldn't explain how they arrived at their conclusions. Neural networks were so complex that their decision-making processes became opaque, raising questions about trust and transparency.

For industries like healthcare, law, and finance, this lack of clarity posed serious ethical concerns. Could society rely on systems it didn't fully understand?

As Alex read about the advancements in machine learning, he felt a growing sense of unease. These systems weren't just tools—they were competitors. They could learn faster, adapt quicker, and outperform humans in ways that seemed almost unfair.

But they weren't perfect. For all their power, AI systems lacked empathy, creativity, and moral judgment. They could make decisions, but they couldn't understand the human consequences of those decisions.

Chapter 5: Industries in Flux

The factory floor was eerily silent. Where there had once been the hum of conversation, the clatter of machinery operated by human hands, and the occasional laughter of workers on break, there was now only the steady rhythm of robotic arms. These machines worked without pause, assembling products with precision humans could never achieve. Efficiency had reached its peak—but at what cost? In the manager's office, an older man sat staring at a report. His factory was now one of the most advanced in the region, with production costs slashed in half. But he couldn't ignore the faces of the workers he had let go, many of whom had been with the company for decades. The gains in profit came with a heavy price: the erosion of the community that had been built around the factory.

AI and automation have disrupted nearly every industry, but some have been more profoundly affected than others. This chapter explores the sectors that have undergone the most significant transformations:

1. Manufacturing

• The Automation Boom: Factories once bustling with activity now operate with skeleton crews. Automated assembly lines, powered by AI, have replaced human workers in industries like automotive, electronics, and textiles.

• Impact: Millions of factory jobs, particularly in developing countries, have disappeared. Communities built around manufacturing hubs have been devastated, leaving workers with limited options.

2. Retail and E-Commerce

- Self-Checkout and Warehousing: Supermarkets and stores increasingly use self-checkout kiosks, while warehouses are staffed by robots that sort, package, and dispatch items with unprecedented speed.

- Impact: Traditional retail jobs, from cashiers to stock clerks, are rapidly vanishing. Meanwhile, e-commerce giants like Amazon dominate, using AI to optimize inventory and predict consumer behavior.

3. Transportation

- The Rise of Autonomous Vehicles: Self-driving trucks, taxis, and delivery drones are becoming the norm. Companies save billions in labor costs, but drivers—once a cornerstone of the workforce—are left scrambling for alternatives.

- Impact: Long-haul truckers, delivery drivers, and taxi operators are some of the hardest-hit groups, facing mass unemployment.

4. Healthcare

- AI Diagnostics and Robotics: AI systems like IBM Watson and robotic surgical assistants have revolutionized healthcare. Machines can now diagnose diseases with accuracy that rivals doctors and perform minimally invasive surgeries.

- Impact: While these technologies improve patient outcomes, they also challenge the roles of radiologists, pathologists, and even general practitioners.

5. Finance and Legal Services

- AI Advisors and Automation: Algorithms now handle tasks like trading, financial planning, and contract review. AI tools can draft legal documents, analyze case law, and predict trial outcomes.

- Impact: Entry-level roles in these fields, once considered secure, are vanishing as AI takes over routine tasks.

Not everyone loses in the era of automation. While some industries and workers are displaced, others thrive:

- Winners:

    - Companies that adopt AI early and strategically.

    - Skilled professionals who design, implement, and maintain AI systems.

    - Consumers, who benefit from lower prices and increased convenience.

- Losers:

    - Workers in repetitive, routine-based roles.

    - Small businesses that can't compete with AI-driven efficiency.

    - Economies reliant on low-skill labor.

This growing divide between winners and losers has widened inequality, creating stark contrasts between those who benefit from AI and those left behind.

The retail industry provides a striking example of how AI reshapes entire sectors.

- Before AI: Retail relied on human cashiers, sales associates, and supply chain managers. Stores were staffed with teams that handled inventory, customer service, and stocking shelves.

- After AI:

    - Inventory management is now handled by algorithms that predict demand with precision.

    - Self-checkout kiosks and automated stores, like Amazon Go, require minimal staffing.

    - Customer interactions are managed by AI chatbots, replacing human representatives.

The result? Lower operational costs and higher profit margins for companies—but at the expense of millions of jobs.

The retail industry provides a striking example of how AI reshapes entire sectors.

- Before AI: Retail relied on human cashiers, sales associates, and supply chain managers. Stores were staffed with teams that handled inventory, customer service, and stocking shelves.

- After AI:

    - Inventory management is now handled by algorithms that predict demand with precision.

- Self-checkout kiosks and automated stores, like Amazon Go, require minimal staffing.

- Customer interactions are managed by AI chatbots, replacing human representatives.

The result? Lower operational costs and higher profit margins for companies—but at the expense of millions of jobs.

While automation has disrupted traditional industries, it has also created new opportunities in fields like:

- AI Development: Engineers, data scientists, and machine learning specialists are in high demand.

- Green Technology: As AI optimizes energy use, jobs in renewable energy and sustainability are growing.

- Creative Roles: Despite AI's capabilities, human creativity remains unmatched in areas like storytelling, art, and design.

However, transitioning into these fields requires significant reskilling, leaving many workers struggling to adapt.

For Alex, the changes weren't just professional—they were deeply personal. Losing his job had shaken his confidence and forced him to reevaluate his place in the world. He wasn't alone. Across the globe, displaced workers shared stories of depression, anxiety, and identity loss.

AI's impact wasn't just economic—it was human. Jobs weren't just sources of income; they were sources of purpose and pride. Without them, people like Alex felt adrift.

Chapter 6: The Human Cost

The town of Brookhaven, once a thriving manufacturing hub, now sat in quiet decline. Abandoned factories stood as grim reminders of the jobs that had disappeared when automation swept through. Main Street, once bustling with shops and diners, was now lined with boarded-up storefronts. Families had moved away in search of opportunities, leaving behind a ghost town where hope seemed to have vanished.

For those who remained, life was a daily struggle. Sarah, a single mother who had worked at the local factory for 15 years, now spent her days applying for jobs and her nights worrying about how to pay rent. Her skills, once in high demand, were no longer relevant in a world dominated by machines.

Losing a job is more than just an economic setback; it's a blow to identity and self-worth. Studies have shown that unemployment can lead to:

- Depression and Anxiety: The uncertainty of not knowing what's next takes a toll on mental health.

- Loss of Purpose: Jobs give people structure and a sense of contribution. Without them, many feel adrift.

- Strain on Relationships: Financial stress often leads to conflicts within families and social circles.

For Sarah, the hardest part wasn't just the lack of income—it was the feeling of being left behind. "I used to be proud of my work," she said, staring at an old photo of her factory team. "Now, I don't know who I am anymore."

The ripple effects of automation aren't confined to individuals; entire communities are affected.

- Economic Decline: Towns and cities dependent on specific industries often face economic collapse when those industries automate.

- Brain Drain: Young people leave in search of opportunities, leaving aging populations behind.

- Erosion of Social Fabric: With fewer jobs, community centers, schools, and local businesses struggle to survive.

Brookhaven was just one example of this global phenomenon. From Rust Belt cities in the United States to industrial towns in Europe and Asia, the story was the same: automation created wealth in some places while leaving others in ruin.

This section presents firsthand accounts of individuals affected by automation:

1. The Factory Worker: Javier, a machinist in Mexico, lost his job to robotic arms imported from abroad. He now works two part-time jobs to make ends meet, barely seeing his family.

2. The Taxi Driver: Priya, a cab driver in Mumbai, saw her income plummet when ride-hailing apps introduced self-driving vehicles.

3.   The Office Professional: Mark, a middle manager in London, was replaced by AI-driven project management software. Now in his 50s, he struggles to compete with younger, tech-savvy candidates.

These stories highlight a common theme: the emotional toll of feeling irrelevant in a world that seems to value efficiency over humanity.

Economists have coined the term "precariat" to describe the growing class of people who live with economic insecurity due to unstable or temporary work. As automation disrupts traditional jobs, the gig economy has filled the gap, offering short-term contracts instead of stable careers.

- Gig Workers: From delivery drivers to freelance designers, these workers lack benefits, job security, and a predictable income.

- Overwork and Underpay: Many gig workers are forced to take on multiple jobs just to cover basic expenses.

- No Safety Net: Without employer-provided benefits like health insurance or pensions, the precariat faces a precarious future.

For Alex, this reality hit hard. After losing his job, he took on gig work to stay afloat. But the pay was low, and the work was inconsistent. "It's like I'm running on a treadmill," he said. "No matter how hard I work, I can't get ahead."

Automation has deepened the gap between those who benefit from technology and those left behind.

- Winners: Highly skilled professionals, entrepreneurs, and tech innovators thrive in this new economy.

- Losers: Low- and middle-income workers in routine-based jobs face growing financial insecurity.

- Resentment and Polarization: This divide fuels political unrest and populist movements, as displaced workers demand change.

Brookhaven's mayor, reflecting on the changes, put it bluntly: "It's hard to ask people to embrace progress when it feels like they're being sacrificed for it."
Despite the challenges, some communities are finding ways to adapt:

1. Retraining Programs: Local governments and nonprofits are offering reskilling opportunities, teaching workers new skills like coding, data analysis, and renewable energy installation.

2. Cooperative Models: Worker-owned businesses are emerging as an alternative to corporate-driven automation.

3. Community Support Networks: Grassroots organizations are stepping in to provide emotional and financial support to displaced workers.

Sarah, for example, enrolled in a free online course in digital marketing. "It's not easy starting over," she said, "but I'm trying to give my kids a future."

Chapter 7: Ethics in AI

A courtroom in the heart of San Francisco was silent as the judge reviewed the final report generated by an AI system. This particular algorithm had been used to recommend sentencing for defendants, analyzing vast amounts of data to predict the likelihood of reoffending. The defendant, a young man named Marcus, had been charged with theft. The AI's recommendation: maximum sentencing.

The defense attorney rose to object, citing studies that showed AI systems often carried hidden biases against minorities. The prosecution countered, arguing that the algorithm was purely objective, basing its decision on data alone. The judge, caught between conflicting arguments, hesitated. In that moment, it was clear: the question wasn't just whether the AI was right—it was whether it could truly be trusted.

AI systems are often touted as impartial, but in reality, they are only as objective as the data they are trained on. When biases exist in the data, AI perpetuates—and sometimes amplifies—them.

- Racial and Gender Bias: Algorithms used in hiring, policing, and lending have been found to discriminate against women and minorities. For example:

    - Facial recognition systems often struggle to identify darker skin tones accurately.

    - Hiring algorithms trained on past data may favor male candidates for technical roles, reflecting historical inequalities.

- **Economic Bias:** Credit scoring systems and loan algorithms can penalize individuals from lower-income backgrounds, perpetuating cycles of poverty.

- **Amplification of Inequality:** Bias in AI doesn't just reflect societal inequalities—it reinforces them, making it harder for marginalized groups to break free.

For Marcus, the defendant in the courtroom, the algorithm's decision wasn't just a recommendation—it was a reflection of a flawed system that valued data over humanity.

The development and deployment of AI are dominated by a handful of tech giants: Google, Amazon, Microsoft, Facebook, and a few others. This concentration of power raises significant ethical concerns:

- **Control Over Data:** These companies collect vast amounts of personal information, often without users fully understanding how their data is used.

- **Monopolization of Innovation:** Smaller companies and startups struggle to compete, stifling diversity and creativity in the AI field.

- **Global Inequality:** Nations without access to cutting-edge AI technology risk falling behind, deepening the divide between developed and developing countries.

The question arises: should a handful of corporations hold so much influence over technology that shapes the future of humanity?

As AI systems become more autonomous, the question of accountability becomes increasingly complex:

- Who is Responsible?: If an AI-powered car causes an accident or an algorithm leads to a wrongful conviction, who should be held accountable—the developers, the operators, or the AI itself?

- The "Black Box" Problem: Many AI systems are so complex that even their creators can't fully explain how they make decisions. This lack of transparency makes accountability difficult.

Governments and regulators are only beginning to grapple with these questions, often lagging far behind the pace of technological advancement.

At its core, the ethical dilemma of AI comes down to one question: *Is it right to replace humans with machines, even if it's more efficient?*

Consider the following scenarios:

1. Healthcare: A robot surgeon can perform procedures with unparalleled precision, but does the absence of human empathy affect patient outcomes?

2. Education: AI tutors can provide personalized learning experiences, but can they inspire and mentor students the way a human teacher can?

3. Art and Creativity: AI-generated music, writing, and art are increasingly indistinguishable from human creations. But does removing the human touch diminish the value of creativity?

In every case, the trade-offs between efficiency and humanity are stark, forcing society to reconsider what it values most.

To address these challenges, a global effort to establish ethical guidelines for AI is underway. Key principles include:

- Transparency: AI systems should be explainable, allowing users to understand how decisions are made.

- Fairness: Efforts must be made to eliminate bias and ensure equitable outcomes for all.

- Accountability: Developers and operators must be held responsible for the consequences of their systems.

- Privacy: Individuals' data must be protected, with clear consent required for its use.

But enforcing these principles is easier said than done. Without global cooperation, companies and countries may prioritize profit and power over ethics.

As Alex read about these issues, he found himself torn. On one hand, the efficiency and innovation brought by AI were undeniable. On the other, the stories of injustice and inequality were impossible to ignore.

One question haunted him: *If AI represents the future, what kind of future are we building?*

Chapter 8: The Divide Widens

On the 43rd floor of a glass-walled skyscraper, Olivia sat in her ergonomic chair, sipping her latte as she reviewed the latest quarterly report. Her tech company had doubled its profits thanks to an AI-driven logistics system that reduced costs and improved efficiency. Below her, the city bustled—but it wasn't the same city she grew up in. The streets were filled with gig workers delivering packages for a fraction of the pay that her father, once a delivery driver, had earned decades earlier.

At the same time, in a small town a few hours away, Dan watched as the last local diner closed its doors. The town had once thrived on factory jobs that were now fully automated. With no tech companies or retraining centers nearby, most of the young people had left, leaving behind an aging population struggling to survive.

Two worlds. Two realities. Both shaped by the same force: AI.

The adoption of AI has fundamentally altered the global economy, dividing society into those who benefit from the technology and those left behind.

- The Winners:

    - Tech Innovators and AI Developers: Companies that create, deploy, and maintain AI systems dominate the global economy, generating immense wealth.

    - Highly Skilled Professionals: Workers with expertise in AI, data science, and software engineering enjoy lucrative careers in high-demand fields.

- Consumers in Developed Nations: People in wealthier countries benefit from cheaper products, faster services, and personalized experiences driven by AI.

- The Losers:

    - Low- and Middle-Skilled Workers: Millions of jobs in manufacturing, retail, and transportation have been automated, leaving workers without viable alternatives.

    - Small Businesses: Many struggle to compete with tech giants that use AI to optimize operations and undercut prices.

    - Developing Countries: Economies reliant on cheap labor face declining demand as automation replaces the need for human workers.

This growing disparity has led to stark inequalities not only between individuals but also between regions, industries, and nations.

AI has reshaped the global economic landscape, concentrating wealth and opportunity in a few key areas:

- Urban Tech Hubs: Cities like San Francisco, Shenzhen, and Bangalore thrive as centers of AI innovation, attracting talent and investment.

- Rural and Industrial Regions: These areas, once reliant on manufacturing and agriculture, face economic stagnation and population decline.

- Developed vs. Developing Nations: Wealthier countries with access to AI research and infrastructure continue to grow, while poorer nations struggle to keep up.

The result is a world where opportunity is increasingly tied to location. For someone like Olivia, living in a tech hub offers endless possibilities. For Dan, trapped in a declining rural town, the future feels bleak.

AI has also widened the gap between the privileged and the marginalized, making it harder for individuals to move up the economic ladder:

- Education: Access to quality education and training programs is critical for success in an AI-driven economy. However, such opportunities are often limited to those who can afford them.

- Reskilling Gaps: Workers displaced by automation often lack the resources or time to learn new skills, leaving them stuck in low-paying, unstable jobs.

- Intergenerational Inequality: Children born into wealthier families have access to the tools and education needed to thrive in the new economy, perpetuating cycles of inequality.

For Alex, the divide became painfully clear as he attended a free reskilling seminar. The course was overcrowded, underfunded, and barely scratched the surface of what he needed to learn. Meanwhile, Olivia's company offered its employees cutting-edge training programs, ensuring they stayed ahead of the curve.

AI has also widened the gap between the privileged and the marginalized, making it harder for individuals to move up the economic ladder:

- Education: Access to quality education and training programs is critical for success in an AI-driven economy. However, such opportunities are often limited to those who can afford them.

- Reskilling Gaps: Workers displaced by automation often lack the resources or time to learn new skills, leaving them stuck in low-paying, unstable jobs.

- Intergenerational Inequality: Children born into wealthier families have access to the tools and education needed to thrive in the new economy, perpetuating cycles of inequality.

For Alex, the divide became painfully clear as he attended a free reskilling seminar. The course was overcrowded, underfunded, and barely scratched the surface of what he needed to learn. Meanwhile, Olivia's company offered its employees cutting-edge training programs, ensuring they stayed ahead of the curve.

Despite the challenges, efforts are underway to reduce the disparities caused by AI:

1. Universal Basic Income (UBI): Some governments and organizations propose UBI as a way to provide financial stability in an era of widespread job displacement.

2.   Public-Private Partnerships: Companies and governments are working together to fund retraining programs and create new job opportunities.

3.   AI for Social Good: Initiatives aim to use AI to address global challenges, such as poverty, healthcare access, and education.

While these efforts offer hope, their impact remains limited compared to the scale of the problem

Closing the divide requires more than goodwill—it demands systemic change:

•   Ethical AI Development: Companies must prioritize fairness, transparency, and inclusivity in their AI systems.

•   Proactive Policies: Governments need to anticipate the impacts of AI and implement policies that support workers and communities.

•   Global Cooperation: Addressing inequalities requires collaboration between nations to ensure that AI benefits everyone, not just a privileged few.

Chapter 9: Reshaping Education

In a brightly lit room filled with holographic displays, a group of students sat at their desks, each immersed in a personalized lesson. The teacher, an AI-driven hologram, moved seamlessly between subjects, adjusting the pace and difficulty of each task to match the individual needs of the students.

For some students, this system was a revelation—offering the kind of tailored education no human teacher could provide. But for others, it lacked the warmth, inspiration, and mentorship that only a human presence could offer.

Outside this futuristic classroom, another reality played out. In a rural town struggling with poverty, a group of children sat on the floor of a dilapidated schoolhouse, using outdated textbooks. The gap between these two classrooms symbolized a growing divide: as technology advanced, access to quality education became increasingly unequal.

AI and automation are rapidly transforming the job market. To prepare individuals for this new reality, education systems must adapt in several key ways:

1. Lifelong Learning:

    •   Jobs are no longer static. Workers must continuously update their skills to remain relevant.

    •   Traditional models of education—where learning ends after college—are no longer sufficient.

2. Focus on Soft Skills:

- While AI excels at technical and repetitive tasks, it struggles with creativity, empathy, and critical thinking.

- Schools must emphasize skills like problem-solving, adaptability, communication, and collaboration.

3. Teaching AI Literacy:

- Understanding how AI works, its limitations, and its ethical implications will be essential for future generations.

- Coding and data analysis should become as fundamental as reading and math.

AI offers exciting opportunities to enhance learning:

- Personalized Learning: AI can tailor lessons to individual students, helping them learn at their own pace.

- Virtual Tutors: Intelligent systems can provide 24/7 assistance, answering questions and offering feedback.

- Gamification: Educational apps and games make learning engaging and interactive.

However, these advancements also raise questions:

- *Will technology replace teachers?*

- *How do we ensure equitable access to these tools?*

- *What happens to the human connection that is central to education?*

While urban schools and wealthy districts have embraced AI-driven education, many rural and underprivileged areas are being left behind:

- Limited Resources: Schools in poorer regions often lack the infrastructure needed to support advanced technologies.

- Digital Divide: Students without access to computers or reliable internet are at a significant disadvantage.

- Teacher Shortages: In struggling areas, the scarcity of qualified teachers compounds the problem.

Efforts to bridge this gap include:

1. Government Investment: Funding for technology in underserved schools.

2. Public-Private Partnerships: Collaborations between tech companies and educational institutions to provide free or low-cost tools.

3. Mobile Solutions: Initiatives like solar-powered tablets and offline educational apps bring learning to remote areas.

As industries evolve, education must prepare students for jobs that don't yet exist. This involves:

- Emphasizing Creativity and Innovation: Jobs in design, entrepreneurship, and the arts will remain uniquely human.

- Encouraging Interdisciplinary Skills: Combining technical knowledge with fields like psychology, ethics, and sociology will be crucial.

- Fostering Resilience: Teaching students to embrace change and uncertainty as opportunities for growth.

For Alex, the need for education reform became personal when his daughter Mia asked, "Daddy, what will I be when I grow up?" He realized that her future job might not even exist yet—and that her ability to adapt would matter more than any specific skill.

Education isn't just for the young. To address the challenges of automation, programs must also focus on adults who need to reskill:

- Accessible Online Learning: Platforms like Coursera and Khan Academy offer flexible options for workers balancing jobs and family responsibilities.

- Government-Subsidized Training: Governments can partner with companies to fund retraining initiatives, especially for displaced workers.

- On-the-Job Training: Companies can invest in upskilling their employees, ensuring they have the tools to thrive in an automated workplace.

Success stories include factories that transitioned workers into robotics maintenance roles and retail employees who became data analysts after completing targeted programs.

As AI takes on a larger role in education, ethical dilemmas arise:

- Bias in Algorithms: Will AI systems perpetuate existing inequalities, favoring students from wealthier or more tech-savvy backgrounds?

- Privacy Concerns: How will student data be collected, stored, and used?

- The Role of Teachers: Should technology supplement or replace educators?

These questions highlight the need for thoughtful implementation to ensure that technology enhances, rather than undermines, the human aspects of learning.

Preparing for an AI-driven future requires a collective effort:

- International Standards: Countries must work together to establish best practices for integrating AI into education.

- Knowledge Sharing: Successful models from one region can be adapted and applied elsewhere.

- Empowering Local Communities: Educational solutions must be tailored to the unique needs of different cultures and regions.

Chapter 10: Policy and Regulation

The chamber was packed as lawmakers debated the introduction of a sweeping new AI regulation bill. On one side, proponents argued for stricter rules to ensure fairness, transparency, and accountability in AI systems. On the other side, critics warned that overregulation could stifle innovation and leave the country lagging behind in the global AI race.

The tension in the room mirrored the broader struggle faced by governments worldwide: how to balance the benefits of AI with the risks it posed to society. As the debate continued, one thing was clear—regulation was no longer optional. It was a necessity.

AI's rapid growth has outpaced the ability of governments to keep up. Without proper oversight, the risks are significant:

1. Bias and Inequality: Unregulated AI systems can perpetuate discrimination and deepen social divides.

2. Loss of Privacy: Massive data collection by AI systems threatens individual privacy and autonomy.

3. Concentration of Power: A few tech giants dominate the AI landscape, raising concerns about monopolies and the erosion of competition.

4. Accountability Gaps: When AI systems make mistakes, it's often unclear who is responsible—developers, operators, or the system itself.

Regulation provides a framework to address these issues, ensuring that AI serves society rather than undermining it.

1. Transparency

- AI systems must be explainable, allowing users to understand how decisions are made.

- Companies should be required to disclose the data used to train their algorithms, as well as potential biases and limitations.

- Example: In healthcare, patients should know why an AI system recommends one treatment over another.

2. Fairness and Inclusion

- Governments can mandate audits to detect and eliminate bias in AI systems.

- Policies should promote diversity in AI development teams, ensuring a broader range of perspectives.

- Example: Hiring algorithms must be monitored to prevent discrimination based on gender, race, or socioeconomic background.

3. Privacy Protection

- Strict data protection laws can limit how companies collect, store, and use personal information.

- Individuals should have the right to control their data, including the ability to opt out of AI-driven systems.

- Example: Regulations like Europe's GDPR provide a blueprint for safeguarding privacy in the digital age.

4. Accountability

- Clear rules must define who is responsible when AI systems cause harm, whether it's a faulty product recommendation or a self-driving car accident.

- Governments can establish AI ethics boards to oversee the deployment of high-risk systems.

Global Challenges in Regulation

1. The AI Arms Race

Countries like the United States, China, and the European Union are competing to dominate AI innovation. This rivalry creates a dilemma:

- Under-Regulation: To stay competitive, countries may avoid imposing strict rules, leading to unchecked risks.

- Over-Regulation: Excessive restrictions could slow innovation and drive talent and investment to less-regulated regions.

2. Cross-Border Issues

AI systems often operate across national borders, making it difficult to enforce regulations. For example:

- How do you regulate a social media platform that collects data in one country and processes it in another?

- How do you hold a foreign company accountable for biased algorithms affecting local users?

Global cooperation is essential to address these challenges, but achieving consensus is far from easy.

Case Study: The EU's AI Act

The European Union is leading the way in AI regulation with its proposed AI Act. Key features include:

- Risk-Based Approach: AI systems are categorized by risk levels (e.g., low-risk, high-risk), with stricter rules for systems with greater potential for harm.

- Prohibited Practices: Certain uses of AI, such as social scoring or exploitative surveillance, are outright banned.

- Transparency Requirements: Users must be informed when they are interacting with an AI system.

While the AI Act has been praised for its comprehensive approach, critics argue that it may place an undue burden on small businesses and startups.

The Role of Public and Private Sectors

Government Responsibility

- Funding Research: Governments can invest in ethical AI research, ensuring that innovation benefits the public good.

- Workforce Development: Policies can support reskilling programs to prepare workers for an AI-driven economy.

- Public Awareness Campaigns: Educating citizens about AI's benefits and risks empowers them to make informed decisions.

Corporate Responsibility

- Ethical Development: Companies must prioritize fairness, transparency, and inclusivity in their AI systems.

- Collaboration with Regulators: Businesses should work with governments to create policies that balance innovation and safety.

- Accountability: Tech companies must take responsibility for the societal impact of their products.

The Path Forward

To build a future where AI benefits everyone, policymakers and developers must work together to address key questions:

- *How do we balance innovation with societal well-being?*

- *What principles should guide the ethical use of AI?*

- *How can global cooperation ensure that AI serves humanity as a whole?*

For Alex, who had recently attended a town hall meeting on AI regulations, these debates felt personal. He wondered whether the policies being discussed would truly protect workers like him or simply serve the interests of tech giants.

Chapter 11: Collaborating with AI

Opening Scene: A New Kind of Partnership

In a bustling hospital, Dr. Elena Torres reviewed patient charts alongside an AI assistant. The system analyzed lab results, flagged potential complications, and even suggested tailored treatment plans. While the AI provided rapid insights, Dr. Torres made the final decisions, using her years of experience and understanding of human emotion to comfort anxious patients.

This partnership between human expertise and machine efficiency exemplified the future of work—one where humans and AI collaborated rather than competed.

As AI continues to evolve, the narrative need not be one of replacement but of partnership. Humans bring qualities that AI cannot replicate: creativity, empathy, ethical reasoning, and a deep understanding of complex social contexts. When combined with AI's speed, precision, and data-processing capabilities, the possibilities for innovation are limitless.

Key reasons collaboration is essential include:

1. Leveraging Strengths: AI excels at repetitive tasks and pattern recognition, while humans thrive in ambiguous and creative problem-solving.

2. Fostering Innovation: Collaborative efforts between humans and AI can lead to breakthroughs in science, healthcare, education, and more.

3. Ensuring Accountability: Humans remain responsible for overseeing AI systems, ensuring ethical use and addressing unintended consequences.

1. Healthcare

- AI's Role: Systems like IBM Watson analyze medical data to assist in diagnoses and suggest treatments.

- Human's Role: Doctors use AI-generated insights as a starting point, combining them with their expertise to deliver compassionate care.

- Outcome: Faster, more accurate diagnoses and improved patient outcomes.

2. Education

- AI's Role: Adaptive learning platforms tailor lessons to individual students, helping them master difficult concepts.

- Human's Role: Teachers provide mentorship, encouragement, and emotional support, addressing each student's unique needs.

- Outcome: A balanced learning experience that combines technology's precision with human connection.

3. Creative Industries

- AI's Role: Tools like generative AI assist artists, writers, and designers by suggesting ideas or creating drafts.

- Human's Role: Creators refine, reinterpret, and infuse their work with personal meaning and emotion.

- Outcome: Enhanced creativity and efficiency without sacrificing authenticity.

As AI takes on more routine tasks, human roles will shift toward areas where emotional intelligence and creativity are crucial. Examples include:

- AI Supervisors: Professionals who monitor and fine-tune AI systems to ensure accuracy and fairness.

- Innovation Specialists: Workers who use AI tools to identify new opportunities and solve complex problems.

- Care and Support Roles: Jobs that require empathy, communication, and personal connection, such as counseling or caregiving.

For Alex, this new landscape of work was both intimidating and exciting. He began exploring courses that focused on collaborative skills, like managing AI systems and integrating them into workflows.

1. Reskilling the Workforce

- Problem: Many workers lack the training needed to transition into collaborative roles.

- Solution: Governments, companies, and educational institutions must invest in accessible, high-quality reskilling programs.

2. Trust in AI

- Problem: Distrust in AI systems, fueled by concerns over bias and transparency, can hinder collaboration.

- Solution: Developers must prioritize explainability and fairness in their designs, while organizations must educate employees on AI's capabilities and limitations.

3. Economic Inequality

- Problem: High-tech tools may only be accessible to well-funded organizations, widening the gap between rich and poor.

- Solution: Public-private partnerships can help democratize access to AI technologies.

Imagine a world where:

- Farmers use AI to predict weather patterns and optimize crop yields.

- Small business owners leverage AI to manage inventory and market their products.

- Scientists and AI collaborate to tackle global challenges like climate change and disease.

In this vision, AI doesn't replace humans—it amplifies their abilities, creating opportunities for growth and innovation.

Practical Steps Toward Collaboration

For Governments

- Fund initiatives that integrate AI into public services, such as healthcare and education.

- Promote policies that encourage collaboration between industries, academia, and the public sector.

For Companies

- Provide training programs to help employees adapt to AI-enhanced workflows.

- Foster a culture of innovation, encouraging employees to experiment with new technologies.

For Individuals

- Embrace lifelong learning, staying curious and open to new tools and methods.

- Focus on building skills that complement AI, such as critical thinking and emotional intelligence.

Chapter 12: The Human Advantage

In a small art studio, Sophia stared at the blank canvas in front of her. She'd spent hours experimenting with ideas and struggling to find inspiration. Her AI assistant offered suggestions, presenting color palettes and designs based on famous artists' styles. Yet, none of the options felt quite right. It wasn't until Sophia stepped away, cleared her mind, and let her imagination wander that the idea hit her—a completely unique, deeply personal vision that no algorithm could ever generate.

It was a reminder: no matter how advanced AI becomes, there are some things only humans can do.

What Makes Humans Irreplaceable?

AI is undeniably powerful, but it has limitations. The following qualities ensure that humans remain essential in an AI-dominated world:

1. Creativity

   • AI can analyze patterns and generate ideas, but it cannot truly innovate or think outside the box.

   • Human creativity stems from personal experiences, emotions, and the ability to combine unrelated concepts in novel ways.

   • Example: A songwriter who draws inspiration from heartbreak or a painter who channels their cultural heritage into their work.

2. Empathy and Emotional Intelligence

   • AI lacks the ability to feel or understand emotions, which are crucial in roles involving human interaction.

- Whether it's a therapist helping a client, a teacher guiding a struggling student, or a doctor comforting a patient, empathy is irreplaceable.

- Example: A nurse holding a patient's hand during a difficult diagnosis, offering reassurance in a way no machine can.

3. Ethical Reasoning

- While AI can follow rules, it cannot navigate complex moral dilemmas or weigh competing values.

- Humans bring context, culture, and ethics into decision-making, which are essential in fields like law, governance, and healthcare.

- Example: A judge considering the societal implications of a ruling beyond the facts presented.

4. Adaptability

- Unlike AI, which relies on training data, humans can adapt to unexpected situations and think on their feet.

- Our ability to pivot in the face of uncertainty makes us resilient and resourceful.

- Example: First responders improvising during a disaster when conditions change rapidly.

5. Cultural and Social Context

- AI struggles to fully understand the nuances of culture, tradition, and history.

- Humans bring a depth of understanding that machines cannot replicate, especially in roles that require cultural sensitivity.

- Example: A diplomat navigating delicate negotiations influenced by centuries of history.

The Value of Imperfection

One of humanity's greatest strengths lies in its imperfections. While AI strives for efficiency and precision, humans find beauty and meaning in flaws:

- Art and Music: Imperfections in a musician's performance can make a song feel raw and emotional.

- Relationships: Human connections are built on vulnerability, misunderstandings, and growth.

- Problem-Solving: Some of the most significant breakthroughs have come from trial and error, rather than a perfect plan.

Our imperfections make us relatable, authentic, and uniquely human.

Case Study: The Role of Storytelling

Storytelling illustrates the human advantage perfectly. While AI can generate narratives, it lacks the ability to craft stories with true emotional resonance. Consider:

- AI-Generated Content: AI can write technically accurate stories, but they often lack depth and originality.

- Human-Crafted Stories: Humans draw from personal experiences, cultural heritage, and emotional insights to create narratives that inspire, educate, and connect.

From ancient myths to modern films, storytelling remains one of humanity's most enduring and irreplaceable art forms.

How Humans Can Leverage Their Strengths

Rather than fearing AI, individuals can focus on amplifying the qualities that set them apart:

1.   Developing Creativity: Engage in hobbies, arts, and projects that encourage innovative thinking.

2.   Building Emotional Intelligence: Practice empathy and active listening to improve relationships and interpersonal skills.

3.   Staying Curious: Lifelong learning helps humans remain adaptable and open to new ideas.

4.   Fostering Collaboration: Work alongside AI to combine human intuition with machine efficiency.

For Alex, this realization was transformative. He began to see AI not as a threat but as a tool to enhance his own unique abilities. By focusing on his creativity and emotional intelligence, he could carve out a role that no machine could replicate.

The future isn't about choosing between humans or AI—it's about finding the right balance:

•   Complementary Roles: Let AI handle routine, data-driven tasks, freeing humans to focus on creativity, strategy, and empathy.

- Mutual Growth: As AI evolves, humans will find new ways to innovate and adapt, ensuring progress continues.

- Preserving Humanity: While technology advances, we must protect the qualities that make us human—our values, emotions, and connections.

Chapter 13: Redefining Success

Emma sat in her garden, sipping tea and reflecting on the choices she had made. Once a high-powered executive, her days had been consumed by meetings, deadlines, and the relentless pursuit of growth. Now, she spent her time tending to her plants, teaching local children about sustainable farming, and writing poetry.

AI had taken over much of her old work, but instead of despairing, Emma had redefined what success meant to her. It wasn't about wealth or status anymore—it was about connection, creativity, and making a difference in her community.

As AI reshapes industries and work, it is also reshaping society's definition of success.

For centuries, success has been tied to:

> 1.   Material Wealth: Owning property, earning a high salary, and acquiring possessions.

> 2.   Career Advancement: Climbing the corporate ladder, earning promotions, and gaining recognition.

> 3.   Productivity: Measuring worth by output and efficiency.

In an AI-driven world, these metrics are being called into question. As machines handle more tasks and create unprecedented efficiency, humans are left to reevaluate what truly matters.

1. Less Time Spent Working

- AI and automation promise to reduce the number of hours humans need to work, offering more time for leisure, creativity, and personal growth.

- However, this shift raises questions:

   - *What will people do with their extra time?*

   - *How will society adapt to a world where work is no longer central to identity?*

2. A Shift in Job Roles

- Jobs of the future will focus on areas where humans excel: creativity, empathy, and strategic thinking.

- Success will depend less on technical skills and more on adaptability, emotional intelligence, and the ability to collaborate with machines.

3. Rising Inequalities

- While some people will thrive in AI-enhanced roles, others may struggle to find purpose in a world where traditional jobs have disappeared.

- Society must redefine success in a way that includes everyone, not just the technologically privileged.

1. Prioritizing Well-Being

- Success will shift from material gain to physical, mental, and emotional well-being.

- More people are adopting lifestyles focused on health, mindfulness, and sustainability.

2. Emphasizing Relationships

- In a world where AI handles much of the work, humans will have more time to strengthen relationships with family, friends, and communities.

- Example: Alex, once consumed by his job, found fulfillment coaching his daughter's soccer team and reconnecting with old friends.

3. Valuing Contribution Over Competition

- Success may be measured by the positive impact individuals have on their communities and the planet.

- Roles in education, caregiving, and environmental stewardship will gain greater recognition.

It's not just individuals who need to rethink success—companies must also adapt.

- Beyond Profit: Organizations will need to prioritize sustainability, ethical practices, and social responsibility alongside financial growth.

- Employee Fulfillment: Companies will focus on creating work environments that foster creativity, purpose, and well-being.

- Community Engagement: Businesses that give back to their communities will gain respect and loyalty from consumers.

Governments play a crucial role in redefining success on a societal level:

- Universal Basic Income (UBI): Providing financial security in an era of widespread job displacement.

• Support for the Arts and Humanities: Funding creative and cultural pursuits to ensure they remain valued in a tech-driven world.

• Infrastructure for Leisure and Learning: Building parks, libraries, and lifelong learning centers to support personal growth.

1. Embracing Diversity

• Success will no longer have a singular definition; it will vary based on individual values, cultures, and circumstances.

2. Celebrating Non-Traditional Paths

• Success stories will include artists, volunteers, and stay-at-home parents, recognizing the value of all contributions.

3. Finding Balance

• The future will emphasize balance between work, play, and personal growth, allowing people to lead richer, more meaningful lives.

Despite these opportunities, the transition won't be easy:

• Cultural Resistance: Many societies still equate success with wealth and status, making change difficult.

• Economic Pressures: Without proper support, displaced workers may struggle to embrace new definitions of success.

• Psychological Barriers: People accustomed to traditional metrics of success may feel lost or inadequate in a changing world.

Alex, for example, found himself grappling with these issues after losing his job. It wasn't until he began volunteering at a local cycling club, mentoring young athletes, that he discovered a new sense of purpose.

Chapter 14: A Hopeful Tomorrow

In a park filled with the sounds of laughter and conversation, families enjoyed a day of leisure. A group of children worked on a robotics project under the guidance of a retired engineer. Nearby, an artist painted a mural that captured the essence of human creativity.

In this world, AI seamlessly supported daily life. Machines handled mundane tasks—ensuring clean streets, efficient transport, and sustainable energy—while humans focused on building connections, creating art, and solving global challenges. It wasn't a utopia, but it was a society that had learned to balance the power of AI with the needs of humanity.

The future of AI doesn't have to be one of conflict or despair. With thoughtful planning, humanity can harness AI to create a world that is:

1.	Equitable

	•	Policies ensure that the benefits of AI are distributed fairly, reducing inequality and providing opportunities for all.

	•	Universal basic income and free access to reskilling programs allow individuals to thrive in an AI-driven economy.

2.	Innovative

	•	Humans and AI collaborate to tackle challenges like climate change, disease, and poverty.

- AI accelerates scientific research, opening new frontiers in medicine, space exploration, and sustainable living.

3. Creative

- With AI taking over repetitive tasks, humans are free to focus on creative and intellectual pursuits.

- Art, music, and storytelling flourish, infused with personal meaning and cultural significance.

4. Connected

- Communities grow stronger as people prioritize relationships and shared experiences over material wealth.

- AI helps bridge cultural divides by fostering understanding and collaboration.

1. Embrace Lifelong Learning

Education becomes a continuous process, empowering individuals to adapt to change and seize new opportunities. Governments, businesses, and individuals invest in:

- Accessible online courses.

- Community-based learning initiatives.

- Platforms that teach not just technical skills but also creativity, ethics, and emotional intelligence.

2. Foster Global Collaboration

Nations come together to establish international agreements on AI ethics, data privacy, and equitable access to technology. This includes:

- Sharing AI advancements with developing nations.

- Creating global standards for AI development and deployment.

- Encouraging cultural exchanges to ensure diverse perspectives shape AI's future.

3. Design AI for Humanity

Developers and companies prioritize ethical, transparent, and inclusive AI systems. Examples include:

- Algorithms designed to eliminate bias and promote fairness.

- AI tools tailored to support marginalized communities.

- Open-source AI projects that empower individuals and small businesses.

As AI takes on more responsibilities, humans will focus on what machines cannot do:

- Building Connections: Strengthening families, communities, and global networks.

- Creating Meaning: Using art, philosophy, and spirituality to explore the deeper questions of existence.

- Leading with Ethics: Guiding AI development in ways that reflect humanity's highest values.

While the vision is hopeful, the path forward will not be without obstacles:

> 1. Resistance to Change: Societies accustomed to traditional structures may struggle to adapt.
>
> 2. Global Inequalities: Ensuring equitable access to AI technologies will require significant effort and cooperation.
>
> 3. Ethical Dilemmas: Balancing innovation with privacy, fairness, and accountability will remain a complex challenge.

But history shows that humanity is resilient. Just as we've adapted to past revolutions, from the Industrial Age to the Information Age, we can navigate the challenges of the AI Age with ingenuity and determination.

As Alex reflected on his journey—from losing his job to discovering a new sense of purpose—he realized that AI hadn't taken his life away; it had given him a chance to reimagine it. By embracing change and focusing on his unique strengths, he had found fulfillment in ways he never thought possible.

The book ends with a call to action:

> • *AI is not the enemy—it's a tool. How we use it will determine the future of our world.*
>
> • *The power to shape this future lies in our hands. Together, we can create a tomorrow where humanity and AI thrive side by side.*

Chapter 15: Preparing the Next Generation

In the quiet of the evening, Maya sat at the kitchen table, watching her son, Liam, build a robot out of spare parts. He struggled with the wiring, his brows furrowed in concentration. She resisted the urge to step in, letting him figure it out on his own. When the robot's arm finally moved, Liam's face lit up with pride.

In that moment, Maya realized that her role wasn't just to provide answers or solutions—it was to nurture the skills and values Liam would need to thrive in a future dominated by AI.

To thrive in an AI-driven world, children need a unique set of skills and values that go beyond traditional education. These include:

> 1.   Critical Thinking: The ability to analyze, question, and evaluate information.

> 2.   Emotional Intelligence: Empathy, communication, and collaboration.

> 3.   Creativity: Thinking outside the box and finding innovative solutions.

> 4.   Adaptability: Embracing change and uncertainty with resilience.

> 5.   Ethical Awareness: Understanding the social and moral impact of technology.

Parents play a crucial role in instilling these traits, starting from a young age.

Encouraging Exploration

- Provide opportunities for hands-on learning through projects, experiments, and real-world challenges.

- Support their natural curiosity by answering questions or helping them research answers together.

- Example: If a child asks why the sky is blue, explore the science behind it together, sparking an interest in physics.

Promoting Problem-Solving

- Give children age-appropriate challenges that require creative thinking and persistence.

- Encourage them to embrace failure as a stepping stone to success.

- Example: Provide building kits or puzzles that require trial and error to complete.

Using Technology as a Tool, Not a Crutch

- Introduce children to coding, robotics, and AI concepts in a playful and engaging way.

- Encourage them to create with technology rather than passively consume it.

- Example: Use platforms like Scratch to teach basic coding or apps like Tynker to build simple games.

Connecting with Nature

- Balance tech time with outdoor activities to foster a sense of wonder and environmental responsibility.

- Example: Take them on hikes, start a family garden, or teach them about renewable energy by building a small solar-powered project.

Modeling Empathy

- Show children how to consider others' feelings and perspectives in daily interactions.

- Encourage them to help others, whether it's through small acts of kindness or volunteering as a family.

Building Communication Skills

- Teach children to express their feelings and listen actively to others.

- Example: Practice resolving conflicts together by discussing how each person feels and brainstorming solutions.

Making Learning Fun

- Create a home environment that celebrates curiosity and exploration.

- Provide access to books, science kits, art supplies, and online resources.

Incorporating Lifelong Learning into Daily Life

- Show your child that learning doesn't stop at school. Take up new hobbies or learn something new together as a family.

- Example: Take online courses together or watch documentaries on topics that interest them.

Discussing AI and Technology

- Introduce children to the basics of AI and its impact on society.

- Discuss the ethical dilemmas posed by AI, such as privacy, bias, and decision-making.

- Example: Talk about how self-driving cars work and ask, "Who should be responsible if an accident happens?"

Encouraging Responsibility

- Teach children to use technology thoughtfully and responsibly.

- Example: Set boundaries for screen time and explain the importance of privacy and consent online.

Creating a Growth Mindset

- Praise effort and persistence rather than just results, reinforcing the idea that challenges help them grow.

- Example: Instead of saying, "You're so smart," say, "I love how hard you worked on this problem!"

Preparing for Uncertainty

- Help children embrace change as an opportunity rather than a threat.

- Example: Share stories of famous innovators who overcame setbacks to achieve success.

Raising a future-ready child isn't about controlling their path but guiding them to discover their own passions and strengths.

- Encourage independence by letting them make decisions and learn from their mistakes.

- Support their interests, even if they don't align with traditional career paths.

Maya learned this when Liam expressed an interest in game design. While she initially wanted him to pursue engineering, she realized that his creativity and passion for storytelling were just as valuable.

Chapter 16: The Role of Schools and Communities

In a brightly lit classroom, students worked in small groups, building robots to solve real-world problems. One group designed a robot to clean plastic from the ocean, while another created a prototype for delivering medical supplies to remote areas. The teacher, no longer lecturing at the front of the room, moved between groups, acting as a mentor and guide.

This wasn't a traditional classroom. It was a space designed to foster collaboration, creativity, and critical thinking—the skills students would need in a world transformed by AI.

Traditional education systems, focused on rote memorization and standardized testing, are ill-suited for preparing children for an AI-driven future. Schools must evolve to:

> 1. Emphasize Skills Over Knowledge: Focus on teaching how to think, solve problems, and adapt, rather than memorizing facts that AI can easily provide.

> 2. Encourage Lifelong Learning: Equip students with the tools and mindset to continue learning throughout their lives.

> 3. Promote Collaboration: Shift from individual achievement to teamwork, reflecting the collaborative nature of future workplaces.

1. Teach AI Literacy

Understanding AI is no longer optional—it's a foundational skill for navigating the modern world.

- Introduce AI Early: Teach students the basics of how AI works, from algorithms to machine learning.

- Focus on Ethics: Discuss the ethical implications of AI, including privacy, bias, and decision-making.

- Hands-On Learning: Use tools like Scratch, Tynker, or LEGO robotics kits to make AI concepts engaging and accessible.

AI is excellent at analyzing data but lacks the ability to innovate or think critically.

- Creative Projects: Encourage students to design solutions to real-world problems, such as sustainability or urban planning.

- Critical Analysis: Teach students to evaluate information, question assumptions, and consider multiple perspectives.

As automation handles routine tasks, emotional intelligence will become a key differentiator for humans.

- Conflict Resolution: Teach students how to navigate disagreements and work through challenges collaboratively.

- Empathy Exercises: Use role-playing or community service projects to help students understand others' perspectives.

The future demands workers who can connect ideas across fields.

- Combine Subjects: Integrate science, technology, engineering, arts, and mathematics (STEAM) into cohesive projects.

- **Real-World Applications:** Show how knowledge from multiple disciplines can solve complex problems, like designing energy-efficient homes or creating smart cities.

Communities can create spaces for lifelong learning, accessible to people of all ages:

- **Makerspaces:** Provide tools and resources for hands-on innovation, such as 3D printers and robotics kits.

- **Libraries of the Future:** Evolve libraries into centers for digital literacy, offering courses in coding, AI, and data science.

Local companies can play a critical role in bridging the gap between education and the workforce:

- **Internships and Mentorships:** Offer students real-world experience and guidance from professionals.

- **Skill-Building Workshops:** Host events where students and workers can learn cutting-edge technologies.

Communities that work together create a strong foundation for children to thrive:

- **Volunteer Programs:** Encourage professionals to volunteer in schools, sharing their expertise in technology, ethics, or creativity.

- **Intergenerational Learning:** Create opportunities for older generations to mentor and teach younger ones, preserving cultural knowledge while embracing new skills.

In this vision, education extends beyond traditional classrooms and includes the entire community:

- Flexible Learning Spaces: Students learn in diverse environments, from labs and museums to nature reserves.

- Collaborative Networks: Schools, businesses, and community organizations work together to design programs that prepare students for the future.

- Global Connections: Technology enables students to collaborate with peers from around the world, fostering cultural exchange and global problem-solving.

1. Finland's Education Revolution

- What They Did: Finland shifted its education system to focus on interdisciplinary, project-based learning.

- Outcome: Students develop critical thinking, collaboration, and problem-solving skills while achieving high academic performance.

2. Makerspaces in Rural India

- What They Did: Nonprofits set up makerspaces in rural villages, teaching children robotics, coding, and design thinking.

- Outcome: Students gained access to opportunities that were previously unimaginable, bridging the digital divide.

While these changes are promising, there are obstacles to overcome:

1. Funding: Many schools lack the resources to implement new technologies or train teachers.

2. Access Inequality: Rural and underprivileged communities often face barriers to educational innovation.

3. Resistance to Change: Teachers and administrators accustomed to traditional methods may be hesitant to adopt new approaches.

Solutions include:

- Public-Private Partnerships: Collaborate with tech companies to provide affordable tools and training.

- Government Grants: Invest in programs that bring cutting-edge education to underserved areas.

- Teacher Training: Provide professional development to help educators adapt to new teaching methods.

Chapter 17: A Future of Lifelong Learning

At the age of 45, Jamal never thought he'd be sitting in front of a computer, attending an online course on AI ethics. As a former factory worker, the idea of learning something so complex felt intimidating. But after losing his job to automation, he realized he needed to adapt. Now, with the help of a government-sponsored program, he was not only learning new skills but also rediscovering the joy of learning. For Jamal, education didn't end when he left school—it was a lifelong journey, one that gave him the tools to reinvent himself in an ever-changing world.

In a future shaped by AI, the need for lifelong learning will be greater than ever. Here's why:

> 1.   Constant Technological Change: As AI continues to evolve, workers will need to regularly update their skills to stay relevant.

> 2.   Longer Career Spans: With people living and working longer, careers will span multiple decades, requiring continuous skill development.

> 3.   Job Market Shifts: Entire industries may disappear, while new ones emerge, creating a demand for adaptable, versatile workers.

Lifelong learning isn't just about survival—it's about personal growth, creativity, and discovering new passions.

1. Flexible Learning Opportunities

Lifelong learning must be accessible to everyone, regardless of age or circumstances:

- Online Courses: Platforms like Coursera, Khan Academy, and Udemy offer flexible, affordable education on a wide range of topics.

- Micro-Credentials: Short, targeted programs allow individuals to gain specific skills without committing to a full degree.

- Workplace Training: Employers can provide ongoing education through workshops, seminars, and mentorship programs.

2. Community Learning Hubs

- Libraries, community centers, and makerspaces can serve as hubs for lifelong learning, offering resources like computers, workshops, and networking opportunities.

- Example: A retired teacher might host free math tutoring sessions, while a local business offers coding workshops for beginners.

In an AI-driven world, individuals must take responsibility for their own education:

- Set Personal Goals: Identify areas of interest or skills you'd like to develop and create a plan to achieve them.

- Explore Resources: From podcasts to YouTube tutorials, there's a wealth of free and accessible learning tools available.

- Stay Curious: Cultivate a mindset of curiosity, seeing every experience as an opportunity to learn.

1. Investing in Reskilling Programs

Governments and organizations must prioritize reskilling initiatives to support workers displaced by automation:

- **Free or Subsidized Education:** Programs like Germany's vocational training system or Singapore's SkillsFuture credits provide models for accessible lifelong learning.

- **Targeted Training:** Focus on skills that are in high demand, such as data analysis, AI ethics, and green technologies.

2. Creating Policies for Lifelong Learning

Governments can encourage lifelong learning by:

- Providing tax incentives for individuals and businesses that invest in education.

- Requiring companies to allocate resources for employee training and development.

- Funding initiatives that bring educational opportunities to underserved communities.

1. Encourage Learning at Any Age

- Break the stigma that education is only for the young. Celebrate stories of older individuals learning new skills and making career transitions.

- **Example:** Highlight a grandmother who learns to code or an artist who starts a second career in AI design.

2. Make Learning Social

- Create opportunities for people to learn together, such as book clubs, study groups, or community challenges.

- Example: A local challenge where participants work on solving real-world problems, like designing a low-cost water purification system.

3. Inspire Through Role Models

- Share stories of lifelong learners who have used education to transform their lives.

- Example: Jamal, the former factory worker, becomes a mentor for others in his community, proving that it's never too late to learn.

Beyond professional advantages, lifelong learning offers personal rewards:

- Boosted Confidence: Learning new skills builds self-esteem and a sense of accomplishment.

- Expanded Horizons: Exposure to new ideas fosters creativity and critical thinking.

- Stronger Social Connections: Learning with others creates opportunities for collaboration and community building.

For Alex, who once felt lost after losing his job, discovering lifelong learning reignited his sense of purpose. He took online courses in data analytics and joined a local cycling club, combining his professional growth with his personal passions.

While the benefits are clear, there are barriers to making lifelong learning universal:

1.   Cost: Many people can't afford the time or money required for education.

2.   Access: Rural areas and underserved communities often lack resources like internet connectivity or local learning hubs.

3.   Mindset: Adults who've been out of school for years may feel intimidated by the idea of returning to learning.

Solutions include:

•   Free or Subsidized Programs: Ensure cost is not a barrier to education.

•   Tech Accessibility: Invest in digital infrastructure to bring online learning to remote areas.

•   Community Outreach: Create welcoming, inclusive spaces that encourage adults to take their first steps back into learning.

Chapter 18: A New Definition of Progress

In a quiet council meeting, city leaders discussed a proposal to transform a vacant industrial area into a green park powered by renewable energy. One council member argued for selling the land to a tech company that promised economic growth, but the community insisted on a different kind of progress—one that prioritized well-being, sustainability, and community connection over pure economic gain.

This shift reflected a broader trend: redefining progress in a world shaped by AI.

For decades, progress has been measured by:

> 1.   Economic Growth: Gross Domestic Product (GDP) is often used as the primary indicator of a nation's success, prioritizing profit over people.

> 2.   Productivity: Societies value efficiency and output, often at the expense of quality of life.

> 3.   Consumption: Progress is equated with consumerism, leading to environmental degradation and unsustainable practices.

In an AI-driven world, these metrics are increasingly inadequate. Machines can deliver unprecedented productivity, but at what cost? Rising inequality, environmental crises, and societal unrest demand a new approach.

1. Prioritizing Well-Being

- Mental and Physical Health: Measure success by the health and happiness of citizens, not just economic output.

- Work-Life Balance: Use AI to reduce working hours, giving people more time to focus on family, hobbies, and personal growth.

2. Sustainability Over Consumption

- Green Technology: Leverage AI to create sustainable systems for energy, agriculture, and urban planning.

- Circular Economy: Shift from a "take-make-waste" model to one that reuses and recycles resources.

3. Community and Connection

- Social Progress: Focus on strengthening communities and fostering connections across cultural and geographic divides.

- Cultural Preservation: Use AI to document and celebrate diverse traditions, languages, and histories.

1. Beyond Profit

- Companies should aim to create social and environmental value alongside financial returns.

- Example: A tech company develops AI tools for affordable healthcare, prioritizing accessibility over profit margins.

2. Employee Well-Being

- AI should be used to reduce workplace stress, automate mundane tasks, and foster creativity.

- Example: A company implements AI systems to handle repetitive paperwork, freeing employees to focus on meaningful projects.

3. Transparent Practices

- Ethical AI development becomes a core measure of success, ensuring fairness, inclusivity, and accountability.

Governments and organizations can adopt new metrics to evaluate societal progress:

- Gross National Happiness (GNH): Focus on well-being, environmental conservation, and cultural preservation.

- Human Development Index (HDI): Measure life expectancy, education, and quality of life alongside economic factors.

- Planetary Boundaries: Assess ecological sustainability, ensuring human activities stay within Earth's limits.

1. Solving Global Challenges

- AI can address critical issues like climate change, poverty, and healthcare access by analyzing data and identifying effective solutions.

- Example: AI models predict the impact of policy changes on carbon emissions, helping governments implement sustainable practices.

2. Promoting Equity

- AI tools can be designed to reduce inequality by improving access to education, healthcare, and financial services.

- Example: An AI-driven app provides free, personalized tutoring to underserved communities.

3. Empowering Local Solutions

- AI enables small communities to innovate and grow by providing tools for local governance, agriculture, and entrepreneurship.

- Example: Farmers in remote areas use AI-powered apps to optimize crop yields and access global markets.

Redefining progress isn't easy and comes with obstacles:

1. Resistance to Change: Governments and businesses accustomed to traditional metrics may resist adopting new frameworks.

2. Inequality in AI Access: Without global cooperation, marginalized communities may struggle to benefit from AI's potential.

3. Balancing Technology and Humanity: Over-reliance on AI risks sidelining human values and connections.

To overcome these challenges, society must adopt a long-term vision that prioritizes sustainability, equity, and well-being over short-term gains.

1. Global Collaboration

- Nations work together to create shared goals for progress, from combating climate change to eradicating poverty.

- Example: An international coalition pools resources to develop AI tools for addressing water scarcity.

2. Empowering the Individual

- Progress is measured not just at a national or global level but by the opportunities and well-being of individuals.

- Example: Governments fund universal access to lifelong learning, enabling everyone to reach their potential.

3. Balancing AI and Humanity

- AI is used as a tool to enhance human life, not replace it. Progress is defined by how well technology serves people, communities, and the planet.

Chapter 19: The Call to Action

In a global summit broadcast across the world, leaders from governments, businesses, and communities gathered to discuss the future shaped by AI. The keynote speaker, a young entrepreneur from a small rural town, shared a powerful story about how AI tools had transformed her community by improving education, enabling sustainable farming, and connecting them to the world.

Her final words echoed across the room:

"AI is not here to decide our future—it's here to help us build it. But we must act with purpose, with vision, and with humanity."

The summit wasn't just a gathering of experts—it was a reminder that everyone has a role to play in shaping the world ahead.

1.   AI is a Tool, Not a Threat

   •   While AI has the potential to disrupt industries and displace jobs, it also offers unprecedented opportunities to enhance human life.

   •   By using AI responsibly, we can amplify our strengths and solve global challenges.

2.   Humanity's Unique Strengths

   •   Creativity, empathy, adaptability, and ethical reasoning are qualities that no machine can replicate.

- The future belongs to those who embrace these strengths and use them to innovate, connect, and lead.

3. Education and Lifelong Learning

- Preparing the next generation for an AI-driven world requires rethinking education, prioritizing critical thinking, emotional intelligence, and adaptability.

- Lifelong learning ensures that individuals remain relevant, curious, and engaged in a rapidly changing world.

4. Redefining Success and Progress

- Success is not just about economic growth or technological advancement; it's about well-being, sustainability, and equity.

- Progress should be measured by the health of our planet, the strength of our communities, and the opportunities available to everyone.

1. Embrace Lifelong Learning

- Take courses, read books, and explore new hobbies to stay adaptable and engaged.

- Example: Enroll in online courses on AI literacy, coding, or creative problem-solving.

2. Develop Emotional Intelligence

- Practice empathy, active listening, and conflict resolution in daily life.

- Example: Join a volunteer group or participate in activities that foster connection and understanding.

3. Advocate for Ethical AI

- Stay informed about how AI is being used in your community and advocate for transparency, fairness, and inclusivity.

- Example: Support organizations working on AI ethics or attend local town halls discussing AI policies.

4. Balance Technology and Humanity

- Use technology thoughtfully, prioritizing meaningful connections and personal growth.

- Example: Limit passive screen time and focus on creative or collaborative tech use.

1. Teach Resilience and Adaptability

- Help children embrace challenges and learn from failure.

- Example: Encourage them to solve puzzles, take risks, and experiment with creative projects.

2. Introduce Technology Responsibly

- Use tools like coding apps, robotics kits, and AI-driven platforms to teach problem-solving.

- Example: Explore projects like building a simple robot or designing an app together.

3. Nurture Values and Ethics

- Discuss the ethical implications of AI and technology, teaching children to think critically about fairness and accountability.

- Example: Talk about real-world scenarios like self-driving cars or AI decision-making in hiring.

1. Build Inclusive Learning Spaces

   - Create hubs like makerspaces and libraries where people can access tools, resources, and workshops.

   - Example: Start a community coding club or sponsor an AI literacy initiative.

2. Encourage Local Innovation

   - Support small businesses and entrepreneurs in using AI to solve local challenges.

   - Example: Partner with local farmers to implement AI-powered tools for sustainable agriculture.

3. Foster Collaboration

   - Bring together schools, businesses, and community leaders to create programs that prepare individuals for the future.

   - Example: Host hackathons or community challenges to address local issues with AI-driven solutions.

1. Invest in Education and Reskilling

   - Fund programs that teach future-ready skills, from coding to creative thinking.

   - Example: Launch free reskilling initiatives for workers displaced by automation.

2. Promote Ethical AI Development

   - Enforce regulations that ensure transparency, fairness, and accountability in AI systems.

- Example: Adopt policies similar to the EU's AI Act, focusing on human-centric design.

3. Measure Progress Holistically

- Shift from GDP to metrics like Gross National Happiness, Human Development Index, and sustainability indicators.

- Example: Develop national reports that highlight progress in education, health, and environmental preservation.

The challenges of an AI-driven future—inequality, displacement, environmental crises—require global cooperation. Nations, corporations, and individuals must work together to:

- Share AI advancements with developing countries to reduce global inequalities.

- Establish international guidelines for ethical AI development.

- Create global platforms for knowledge sharing and collaborative problem-solving.

Introduction: AI in the Real World

This chapter highlights successful implementations of AI in various sectors, showcasing both its transformative potential and the challenges it brings. By examining these case studies, readers gain a deeper understanding of how AI is shaping industries, communities, and lives.

Case Study 1: AI in Agriculture – Feeding the World

Setting the Scene: In a rural village in India, farmers are facing unpredictable weather patterns caused by climate change. Crop yields have dwindled, and many families struggle to make ends meet. Enter AI-powered tools like Plantix and Agribot, which analyze soil health, weather forecasts, and crop conditions to provide farmers with actionable insights.

The Solution:

• Farmers use an AI app to take photos of crops, and the system diagnoses diseases, suggesting treatments.

• Drones equipped with AI sensors monitor fields for pest infestations, applying targeted pesticide sprays only where needed.

• Machine learning models predict optimal planting times and water usage, maximizing efficiency and minimizing waste.

The Results:

• Farmers in the village see a 30% increase in crop yields within a year.

- Pesticide use drops by 40%, reducing costs and environmental damage.

- Younger generations, previously reluctant to follow in their parents' footsteps, are now excited to embrace tech-enabled farming.

Challenges and Insights:

- Accessibility: Many farmers lacked smartphones or internet access initially, requiring partnerships with local governments to bridge the gap.

- Trust: Convincing farmers to adopt unfamiliar technology was a hurdle, overcome through community workshops and demonstrations.

Case Study 2: AI in Healthcare – Saving Lives in Remote Areas

Setting the Scene: In a remote region of Sub-Saharan Africa, access to doctors is limited, with patients often traveling days to receive care. AI-powered healthcare tools like Babyl (a telemedicine app) and AI diagnostic systems revolutionize access to medical services.

The Solution:

- Patients use smartphones to consult AI chatbots for preliminary diagnoses, receiving advice on whether to treat symptoms at home or seek medical attention.

- AI algorithms analyze X-rays and scans sent from local clinics, providing results in minutes instead of weeks.

- Drones deliver essential medicines to remote areas, bypassing poor infrastructure.

The Results:

- Medical services become accessible to over 100,000 residents, with AI correctly identifying common conditions like malaria and pneumonia with 90% accuracy.

- Maternal and infant mortality rates drop significantly due to faster access to healthcare.

Challenges and Insights:

- Language Barriers: AI systems had to be trained in local dialects to ensure effective communication.

- Ethical Concerns: Privacy and data security were critical considerations when storing patient data in cloud systems.

Case Study 3: AI in Education – Closing the Gap

Setting the Scene: In a low-income urban neighborhood in Brazil, students face overcrowded classrooms and a lack of resources. AI-powered platforms like Khan Academy and local initiatives like Geekie Labs step in to provide personalized learning experiences.

The Solution:

- Students use adaptive learning apps that assess their strengths and weaknesses, tailoring lessons to their needs.

- Teachers receive AI-generated insights about student performance, helping them identify those who need extra support.

- Virtual tutors assist students with homework, offering explanations in their native language.

The Results:

- Test scores improve by 20% in one year, with previously struggling students showing the most significant gains.

- Dropout rates decrease as students gain confidence in their abilities and feel more engaged.

Challenges and Insights:

- Infrastructure: Many schools initially lacked computers, requiring investment in hardware and internet access.

- Teacher Training: Educators needed support to integrate AI tools effectively into their classrooms.

These case studies highlight how AI, when used thoughtfully, can address some of the world's most pressing challenges. However, they also reveal the importance of ensuring accessibility, equity, and ethical implementation.

Chapter 21: The Ethical Dilemmas of AI

A Double-Edged Sword

As AI integrates deeper into society, it brings immense benefits—but also profound ethical challenges. From biased algorithms to privacy concerns, the dilemmas posed by AI are as complex as the technology itself. This chapter explores these issues and the moral questions we must address to ensure AI is a force for good.

1. Bias in AI: A Flawed Mirror

The Problem

AI systems are only as unbiased as the data they're trained on, and that data often reflects existing societal prejudices.

- Example: A hiring algorithm trained on historical company data may favor male candidates because past hiring practices were biased against women.

- Example: Facial recognition systems often perform poorly on darker skin tones due to underrepresentation in training datasets.

Real-World Impacts

- Discrimination in Hiring: Job applicants from minority groups may be unfairly filtered out.

- Unfair Policing: Predictive policing algorithms may disproportionately target marginalized communities.

Solutions and Considerations

- Diverse Training Data: AI developers must ensure datasets are representative of all demographics.

- Bias Audits: Regularly audit AI systems to detect and mitigate bias.

- Human Oversight: Include diverse teams in AI development to bring varied perspectives and reduce blind spots.

2. Privacy: The Cost of Convenience

The Problem

AI relies on massive amounts of personal data, raising concerns about how that data is collected, stored, and used.

- Example: Social media platforms use AI to analyze user behavior and deliver targeted ads, often without clear consent.

- Example: Smart home devices like Alexa and Google Home continuously collect audio data, raising questions about surveillance.

Real-World Impacts

- Data Breaches: Sensitive information can fall into the wrong hands, leading to identity theft or financial fraud.

- Loss of Autonomy: Users may feel they're constantly being monitored, eroding trust in technology.

Solutions and Considerations

- Transparent Policies: Companies must clearly explain how they collect and use data.

- Data Minimization: Collect only the data necessary for AI to function effectively.

- Privacy-Enhancing Technologies: Invest in tools like differential privacy and encryption to protect user data.

3. AI in Warfare: Ethical Boundaries

The Problem

The use of AI in autonomous weapons and military operations raises moral questions about accountability and human oversight.

- Example: Autonomous drones capable of identifying and eliminating targets without human intervention blur the lines of responsibility.

- Example: AI-powered cyberattacks can cause widespread disruption, targeting critical infrastructure like power grids or hospitals.

Real-World Impacts

- Loss of Human Control: Decisions about life and death may be left to machines.

- Escalation of Conflict: AI could lower the threshold for war by making it easier to deploy automated systems.

Solutions and Considerations

- International Agreements: Establish global treaties to regulate the development and use of AI in warfare.

- Human Oversight: Ensure humans remain in control of all lethal decision-making processes.

- Ethical Design: Develop AI systems that align with international humanitarian laws.

4. Accountability: Who is Responsible?

The Problem

When AI systems cause harm, it's often unclear who should be held accountable—the developer, the operator, or the AI itself.

- Example: If a self-driving car causes an accident, is the blame on the manufacturer, the programmer, or the car owner?

Real-World Impacts

- Legal Gaps: Current laws struggle to address the complexities of AI accountability.

- Public Distrust: Without clear accountability, people may lose confidence in AI systems.

Solutions and Considerations

- Clear Guidelines: Governments must establish laws defining liability in AI-related incidents.

- Transparent Systems: Developers should design AI systems that can explain their decisions, making it easier to identify failures.

- Ethical Certification: Create standards and certifications for AI systems to ensure accountability.

5. Manipulation and Misinformation

The Problem

AI-driven tools are increasingly being used to manipulate public opinion and spread misinformation.

- Example: Deepfake videos can create convincing yet fake content that damages reputations or spreads false narratives.

- Example: Social media algorithms amplify divisive content to maximize engagement, fueling polarization.

Real-World Impacts

- Erosion of Trust: People struggle to distinguish between real and fake information.

- Political Instability: Manipulated content can influence elections and destabilize governments.

Solutions and Considerations

- AI for Verification: Use AI to detect and flag manipulated content.

- Platform Accountability: Social media companies must take responsibility for monitoring and removing harmful content.

- Media Literacy: Educate the public on how to identify and avoid misinformation.

6. The Ethics of AI Ownership

The Problem

AI is largely controlled by a few tech giants, raising concerns about monopolies and unequal access.

- Example: Companies like Google and Amazon dominate AI research, leaving smaller organizations and developing nations at a disadvantage.

Real-World Impacts

- Global Inequality: Developing countries may struggle to access AI technologies, widening the gap between rich and poor nations.

- Lack of Competition: Concentrated ownership stifles innovation and reduces consumer choice.

Solutions and Considerations

- Open-Source AI: Promote open-source AI tools to democratize access.

- Public Investment: Governments and nonprofits can fund AI projects that prioritize societal benefit over profit.

- Antitrust Regulations: Enforce laws to prevent monopolistic practices in the AI industry.

Conclusion: Navigating Ethical Dilemmas

This chapter ends with a call to action for all stakeholders:

- Developers: Design AI systems that prioritize fairness, transparency, and inclusivity.

- Governments: Implement regulations that protect individuals and promote ethical AI use.

- Individuals: Stay informed about AI's ethical implications and advocate for responsible practices.

Chapter 22: Preparing Society for AI

A Collective Responsibility

As AI continues to reshape industries and societies, the responsibility to prepare for its impact doesn't fall on one group—it's shared by individuals, communities, governments, and organizations. This chapter explores practical strategies for ensuring that society is equipped to adapt, thrive, and maintain its humanity in an AI-driven world.

1. Building Public Awareness

The Problem

Many people lack an understanding of what AI is, how it works, and how it impacts their lives. This knowledge gap can lead to fear, misinformation, and resistance to change.

Solutions

- AI Literacy Campaigns: Launch public awareness programs to educate people about AI, focusing on its benefits, risks, and limitations.

  - Example: Governments and tech companies collaborate on free workshops and online resources about AI basics.

- Accessible Media: Create documentaries, podcasts, and books that simplify AI concepts for the general public.

- Community Discussions: Host town halls and forums where people can ask questions and share concerns about AI.

2. Empowering Communities

The Problem

Communities, particularly in rural and underserved areas, often lack access to the tools and resources needed to adapt to AI advancements.
Solutions

- Localized Learning Hubs: Establish community centers equipped with AI tools, internet access, and educational resources.

  - Example: A small-town library hosts coding workshops and provides access to AI-powered learning platforms.

- Community-Led Innovation: Encourage grassroots projects where local residents use AI to solve specific problems, such as optimizing water usage or creating job opportunities.

- Collaborative Networks: Create regional alliances where communities share resources, knowledge, and best practices for integrating AI.

3. Transforming the Workforce
The Problem
Millions of jobs are at risk of being replaced by automation, leaving workers vulnerable to unemployment and economic instability.
Solutions

- Reskilling and Upskilling Programs: Provide workers with training in future-proof skills like data analysis, AI ethics, and digital marketing.

- Example: A government program partners with tech companies to offer free online courses for displaced workers.

- Career Transition Support: Offer counseling and mentorship to help individuals navigate career changes caused by automation.

- Job Creation in Emerging Fields: Promote growth in industries where human skills—like empathy, creativity, and ethical reasoning—remain essential.

4. Rethinking Education

The Problem

Traditional education systems are not designed to prepare students for the unique challenges and opportunities of an AI-driven world.

Solutions

- AI-Integrated Curriculums: Teach AI literacy and ethical reasoning as core subjects alongside math and language.

- Project-Based Learning: Replace rote memorization with hands-on projects that develop creativity, critical thinking, and collaboration.

- Lifelong Learning Pathways: Design education systems that support continuous learning, allowing individuals to acquire new skills at any stage of life.

5. Bridging the Digital Divide

The Problem

Many communities lack the infrastructure and access needed to benefit from AI technologies, widening inequality.

Solutions

- Invest in Infrastructure: Governments must prioritize expanding internet access and providing affordable technology to underserved areas.

    - Example: Rural broadband initiatives ensure that remote villages have access to online education and resources.

- Public-Private Partnerships: Collaborate with tech companies to donate devices and fund connectivity projects.

- Localized Solutions: Develop offline AI tools that can function in areas with limited internet access.

6. Shaping Policies and Regulations

The Problem

Without proactive policies, AI can exacerbate inequality, threaten privacy, and lead to misuse.

Solutions

- Ethical Guidelines: Governments should adopt frameworks that ensure AI systems are transparent, fair, and inclusive.

- Universal Basic Income (UBI): Consider implementing UBI as a safety net for individuals displaced by automation.

- Global Cooperation: Work with other nations to create international agreements on AI ethics, data privacy, and responsible development.

7. Fostering Global Solidarity

The Problem

AI benefits are often concentrated in wealthier nations, leaving developing countries behind.
Solutions

- Technology Sharing: Create programs that provide AI tools and resources to developing countries.

  - Example: Open-source AI platforms tailored for agriculture, healthcare, and education in low-resource settings.

- Capacity Building: Train local talent in developing nations to create and implement AI solutions.

- Global Initiatives: Form international coalitions to address challenges like climate change, poverty, and healthcare using AI.

8. Promoting Ethical AI Development

The Problem

Unchecked AI development can lead to bias, misuse, and unintended harm.
Solutions

- Ethics in AI Education: Require all AI developers and researchers to study ethics as part of their training.

- Independent Oversight: Establish third-party organizations to audit and certify AI systems for fairness and safety.

- Accountability Measures: Ensure developers and organizations are held accountable for the impact of their AI systems.

9. Encouraging Public Participation

The Problem

People often feel powerless to influence decisions about AI, leaving important debates to experts and corporations.
Solutions

- Citizen Panels: Involve citizens in decision-making processes about AI policies and projects.

  - Example: A city council creates a public advisory board to discuss the implementation of AI in public services.

- Accessible Feedback Channels: Allow individuals to voice concerns and suggestions about AI systems in their communities.

- Educational Campaigns: Empower individuals to understand and advocate for their rights in an AI-driven world.

Conclusion: A Shared Mission

Preparing society for AI isn't just about adapting to change—it's about shaping it. With collaboration, foresight, and a commitment to inclusivity, we can create a future where AI enhances human life rather than undermining it.

A New Era of Expression

In a bustling art studio, an artist collaborated with an AI assistant to create a vivid mural. While the AI suggested colors and patterns based on historical masterpieces, the artist infused the piece with personal meaning and cultural symbolism. Together, they created something neither could have achieved alone.

This scene reflects a growing trend: AI is transforming creativity, not by replacing artists, writers, and musicians but by expanding the possibilities of human expression.

1. How AI is Revolutionizing the Creative Process

Visual Arts

- Generative Art: AI tools like DALL·E and DeepDream enable artists to generate intricate designs and explore new visual styles.

  - Example: An artist uses AI to create abstract landscapes that evolve based on user interactions.

- Restoration and Curation: AI helps restore damaged artwork and analyze historical pieces for authenticity.

  - Example: Museums use AI to recreate faded Renaissance murals, preserving cultural heritage.

Music

- AI Composers: Tools like AIVA and Amper Music generate original compositions in various genres.

- Example: A film director collaborates with AI to create a custom soundtrack tailored to the mood of each scene.

- Enhancing Creativity: Musicians use AI to experiment with melodies, harmonies, and arrangements.

  - Example: A producer uses AI to remix a song with entirely new instrumentation.

Writing

- AI-Assisted Writing: Platforms like ChatGPT help authors brainstorm ideas, generate outlines, and edit drafts.

  - Example: A novelist overcomes writer's block by collaborating with AI to explore alternative plotlines.

- Content Creation: AI automates routine writing tasks, such as generating news articles or product descriptions.

2. The Benefits of AI in Creativity

Amplifying Human Potential

- Speed and Efficiency: AI automates repetitive tasks, allowing creators to focus on their vision.

  - Example: Graphic designers use AI to generate quick mockups, speeding up the creative process.

- Breaking Creative Barriers: AI tools inspire new ideas by analyzing patterns, trends, and possibilities beyond human intuition.

  - Example: AI suggests unconventional color combinations for a painting, leading to a groundbreaking style.

Accessibility

- Empowering Amateurs: AI democratizes creativity by providing easy-to-use tools for non-professionals.

  - Example: A high school student uses AI to produce professional-quality music from their laptop.

- Global Collaboration: AI enables creators from different cultures to collaborate in real-time, transcending language barriers.

3. The Challenges of AI in Creativity

Loss of Authenticity

- Critics argue that AI-generated art lacks the emotional depth and personal touch of human-made work.

  - Example: A digital painting created entirely by AI sparks debate about whether it can truly be called "art."

Intellectual Property Issues

- AI systems trained on existing works raise questions about copyright and originality.

- Example: An AI-generated song closely resembles a copyrighted track, leading to legal disputes.

Over-Reliance on AI

- There's a risk that creators may depend too heavily on AI, stifling human innovation and experimentation.

- Example: A screenwriter relies on AI to generate scripts, leading to formulaic storytelling.

4. The Role of Humans in AI-Driven Creativity

The Human Touch

- Emotional resonance, cultural context, and personal experience are qualities only humans can bring to creative works.

- Example: A poet combines AI-generated metaphors with their own lived experiences to craft a deeply moving piece.

Curators and Collaborators

- In the future, creators may act more as curators, guiding and refining AI-generated ideas.

- Example: An architect uses AI to generate building designs but selects and modifies those that align with their vision.

Ethical Guardians

- Creators must ensure that AI-generated works respect cultural traditions, avoid harmful stereotypes, and promote inclusivity.

- Example: A filmmaker uses AI to create diverse characters but reviews the output for potential bias.

5. AI and the Future of Cultural Preservation

Documenting Traditions

- AI can record and analyze endangered languages, rituals, and art forms, preserving them for future generations.

  - Example: AI-powered apps document Indigenous storytelling traditions, making them accessible worldwide.

Reviving Lost Art

- AI reconstructs lost or incomplete works of art, offering new insights into history.

  - Example: Scholars use AI to complete an unfinished symphony by a 19th-century composer.

6. How AI Changes the Definition of Creativity

As AI becomes a collaborator in the creative process, it challenges traditional notions of authorship and originality:

- Collaboration Over Individuality: Creativity becomes a partnership between humans and machines.

- Process Over Product: The act of creating, rather than the final result, takes center stage.

- Redefining Originality: AI blurs the lines between inspiration and imitation, forcing society to reconsider what it means to create something "new."

7. Ensuring Creativity Thrives in an AI World

Education and Training

- Teach students how to use AI tools effectively while emphasizing critical thinking and originality.

    - Example: Art schools offer courses on AI-assisted design alongside traditional techniques.

Support for Human Artists

- Governments and organizations can provide grants, residencies, and platforms that celebrate human creativity.

    - Example: A national arts foundation funds projects that explore the intersection of AI and traditional crafts.

Ethical AI Development

- Developers must design AI systems that empower, rather than overshadow, human creators.

    - Example: AI tools are programmed to prioritize collaboration, offering suggestions without dominating the creative process.

Chapter 24: Reshaping Global Collaboration with AI

A Connected World
In a bustling market in Ghana, a farmer consults an AI-powered app to get real-time market prices for her produce. Thousands of kilometers away, a small business owner in Italy uses a similar platform to analyze global demand for his handmade leather goods. Although these individuals have never met, they are connected through AI-driven tools that break down barriers and enable global collaboration.

AI is reshaping how people, industries, and nations work together, creating unprecedented opportunities for cooperation in solving global challenges.

1. AI as a Bridge Across Cultures
Breaking Language Barriers

- AI-powered translation tools like Google Translate and DeepL enable seamless communication between people who speak different languages.

    - Example: A teacher in Japan collaborates with educators in South America to design a global sustainability curriculum using AI translation tools.

Preserving Cultural Diversity

- AI is being used to document and revitalize endangered languages and traditions.

    - Example: Apps powered by AI record and teach Indigenous languages to younger generations.

Facilitating Global Collaboration

- AI platforms connect professionals and organizations from around the world, fostering knowledge-sharing and innovation.

  - Example: Scientists from different countries use AI tools to collaborate on climate change research in real time.

2. AI in International Trade and Development

Optimizing Global Supply Chains

- AI analyzes shipping routes, market trends, and consumer demands to improve the efficiency of international trade.

  - Example: An AI system predicts delays in shipping goods from Asia to Europe, allowing businesses to adjust their schedules and reduce costs.

Empowering Small Businesses

- AI-driven e-commerce platforms help small businesses reach global markets.

  - Example: A craftsperson in Kenya uses an AI platform to market handmade jewelry to customers in Europe and North America.

Reducing Economic Inequalities

- AI tools provide developing nations with access to resources and information that level the playing field.

- Example: Farmers in rural India use AI to predict weather patterns and optimize crop yields, boosting local economies.

3. Global Challenges Addressed Through AI Collaboration

Climate Change

- AI models predict the impact of environmental policies, monitor deforestation, and optimize renewable energy systems.

  - Example: AI-powered satellites track carbon emissions, helping governments enforce international agreements on climate action.

Healthcare

- AI accelerates the development of vaccines, diagnoses diseases in remote areas, and improves healthcare delivery.

  - Example: AI algorithms analyze global health data to predict and prevent the spread of pandemics.

Humanitarian Aid

- AI systems optimize disaster response, distribute resources efficiently, and predict areas at risk of crises.

  - Example: During a natural disaster, AI-powered drones deliver food and medical supplies to remote regions.

4. The Role of Governments in AI Collaboration

Creating Global Frameworks

- Nations must work together to establish regulations that ensure AI is used ethically and equitably.

- Example: An international AI treaty sets standards for data privacy, bias prevention, and responsible AI development.

Sharing Technology

- Wealthier nations can share AI tools and expertise with developing countries to address inequalities.

- Example: A global initiative trains engineers in low-income countries to develop and implement AI solutions tailored to local needs.

Preventing an AI Arms Race

- Collaborative agreements can prevent the misuse of AI in military applications and promote peace.

- Example: The United Nations facilitates a treaty banning fully autonomous weapons systems.

5. Industry and Academia Driving Collaboration

Cross-Border Research Initiatives

- Universities and research institutions partner globally to advance AI technologies.

- Example: Researchers in the US and South Korea collaborate on AI-powered prosthetics that adapt to individual users.

Open-Source AI

- Open-source platforms democratize AI development, allowing anyone to contribute and benefit.

- Example: Developers from multiple countries improve an open-source AI tool for detecting crop diseases.

Corporate Partnerships

- Companies across industries form alliances to address shared challenges.

    - Example: Tech firms partner with nonprofits to create AI solutions for clean water access in drought-prone regions.

6. Challenges to Global AI Collaboration

Technological Inequality

- Unequal access to AI tools and infrastructure risks widening the gap between developed and developing nations.

Ethical Conflicts

- Different cultural and political values can create disagreements over how AI should be used.

Data Sovereignty

- Concerns about who owns and controls data can hinder international cooperation.

Mistrust Between Nations

- Geopolitical tensions may limit the sharing of AI advancements and data.

7. Solutions to Foster Collaboration

Building Trust

- Transparency and clear communication are essential to fostering trust between nations, organizations, and communities.

Inclusive AI Development

- Involve diverse voices from different regions, industries, and cultures in AI decision-making processes.

Global Education and Awareness

- Promote AI literacy worldwide, ensuring that people everywhere understand and benefit from the technology.

Investing in Infrastructure

- Develop global partnerships to build digital infrastructure in underserved areas.

- *AI has the power to bring the world closer together, addressing shared challenges and creating opportunities for everyone.*

- *To realize this potential, we must prioritize collaboration, equity, and mutual respect, ensuring that no one is left behind in the AI-driven future.*

"AI and Us: Navigating the Future of Work, Creativity, and Ethics"

The Question of Humanity

In a quiet room, a programmer watches as an AI-generated painting sells for millions of dollars at an auction. Across the world, a robotic caregiver comforts an elderly woman in a nursing home, offering words of reassurance. These moments provoke deep questions: *What does it mean to be creative? To care? To be human?*

As AI becomes increasingly capable, it challenges our understanding of humanity and raises profound philosophical questions about consciousness, creativity, and the essence of existence.

1. The Nature of Creativity

Can AI Truly Create?

AI systems can generate art, music, and literature, but does this qualify as true creativity?

- AI's Strengths:

    - AI analyzes vast datasets, identifies patterns, and combines elements to create something new.

    - Example: AI-generated symphonies mimic the styles of Mozart and Beethoven.

- The Human Element:

    - Human creativity is driven by emotion, experience, and intention—qualities AI lacks.

- Example: A poet writes about heartbreak, infusing their work with deeply personal meaning that AI cannot replicate.

The Debate

Some argue that creativity is the ability to produce something original and valuable, a definition AI can meet. Others believe creativity is inherently tied to human consciousness and emotion.

2. Consciousness and Sentience

What Is Consciousness?

- Consciousness is the awareness of one's existence, thoughts, and emotions. While humans possess this quality, AI does not.

- The Hard Question: Can an entity without consciousness truly understand or experience the world?

The Future of AI and Sentience

- Current AI: AI operates based on algorithms and data; it doesn't feel or think independently.

- Speculative AI: Futurists debate whether AI could one day achieve sentience through advanced neural networks.

Ethical Implications

If AI were to develop consciousness, would it deserve rights or protection? How would this change our relationships with machines?

3. The Value of Imperfection

The Human Advantage

- Human beings are imperfect, and these imperfections—flaws, mistakes, and vulnerabilities—are central to our identity.

  - Example: A jazz musician improvises a melody that deviates from the planned piece, creating something unique and unexpected.

AI's Precision

- AI excels at precision, logic, and efficiency, but it lacks the capacity to embrace or value imperfection.

  - Example: An AI composer produces flawless music, but critics argue it lacks the raw emotion of a human performance.

The Philosophical Question

Does imperfection make us human, and if so, how does AI's perfection challenge our sense of identity?

4. Relationships with Machines

Can Machines Form Relationships?

- AI-powered systems like virtual companions and robotic caregivers simulate human interaction, but do they truly form relationships?

  - Example: An elderly woman bonds with her robotic pet, feeling comforted and less lonely.

The Debate

- Supporters: AI companions provide emotional support, especially for individuals who are isolated or vulnerable.

- Critics: These interactions are ultimately one-sided, as machines lack genuine feelings or empathy.

The Ethical Question

Should society encourage relationships with machines, or does this risk undermining authentic human connections?

5. The Role of AI in Redefining Humanity

Expanding Our Understanding

- As AI takes on tasks traditionally associated with humans—creativity, caregiving, problem-solving—it forces us to reconsider what makes us unique.

The Evolution of Humanity

- Some argue that humanity's defining trait is not what we do, but our capacity to adapt, grow, and redefine ourselves.

  - Example: The Industrial Revolution didn't make humans obsolete; it redefined work and progress.

The Philosophical Perspective

Instead of fearing AI's capabilities, we can view them as an opportunity to focus on qualities that truly define humanity: empathy, ethical reasoning, and the ability to dream.

6. The Future of Coexistence

A Partnership with AI

- Rather than competing with machines, humans and AI can collaborate to achieve greater innovation and understanding.

  - Example: AI assists researchers in decoding ancient texts, while human scholars interpret their cultural significance.

Preserving Humanity

- To maintain our humanity, we must prioritize relationships, creativity, and ethical responsibility in a world increasingly influenced by technology.

The Big Question

In a future where machines can do so much, what role will humans play? The answer lies in embracing what makes us unique and irreplaceable.

AI challenges us to reflect on what it means to be human, but it doesn't diminish our value. Instead, it provides an opportunity to rediscover and celebrate the qualities that define us: our creativity, empathy, and capacity for growth.

Chapter 26: Building an AI-Driven Future We Can Trust

In a world increasingly shaped by AI, trust is the cornerstone of progress. Without trust, people hesitate to adopt new technologies, governments delay policies, and businesses lose credibility. This chapter focuses on how we can build a future where AI is safe, inclusive, and beneficial for all.

1. The Foundations of Trust in AI

Transparency

- AI systems must be explainable, allowing users to understand how decisions are made.

  - Example: A healthcare AI should provide clear explanations for why it recommends a particular treatment plan.

- Strategies for Transparency:

  - Use interpretable algorithms that clearly document their decision-making process.

  - Provide users with access to "explainability reports" that detail how AI systems operate.

Fairness

- AI systems should treat all individuals equitably, avoiding discrimination or bias.

  - Example: Hiring algorithms must be designed to avoid favoring one demographic group over another.

- Strategies for Fairness:

- Regularly audit datasets to identify and remove biases.

- Involve diverse teams in AI development to minimize blind spots.

Accountability

- Clear guidelines must define who is responsible when AI systems fail or cause harm.

  - Example: If a self-driving car causes an accident, the manufacturer, operator, or both should be held accountable.

- Strategies for Accountability:

  - Establish legal frameworks that outline liability in AI-related incidents.

  - Require companies to publish impact assessments for high-risk AI systems.

2. Ensuring Safety and Security
Protecting Against Malfunctions

- AI systems must be rigorously tested to prevent errors or failures in critical applications.

  - Example: An AI used in air traffic control must undergo extensive simulation testing before deployment.

Cybersecurity

- AI systems must be protected from hacking or malicious misuse.

- Example: Hackers manipulating an AI-driven stock trading algorithm could destabilize financial markets.

- Strategies for Security:

  - Use encryption and advanced cybersecurity measures to protect AI systems.

  - Implement continuous monitoring to detect and respond to threats.

3. The Role of Governments and Regulations

Proactive Policies

- Governments must create regulations that keep pace with AI development, prioritizing safety and fairness.

  - Example: The EU's AI Act categorizes AI systems by risk levels, imposing stricter rules on high-risk applications like facial recognition.

- Key Areas for Regulation:

  - Data privacy and consent.

  - Ethical use of AI in public services.

  - Restrictions on autonomous weapons and other dangerous technologies.

Global Cooperation

- AI impacts are global, requiring international collaboration to create consistent standards.

- Example: A global treaty could establish shared guidelines for ethical AI use and data privacy.

- Strategies for Collaboration:

    - Create international forums where countries share knowledge and best practices.

    - Encourage cross-border partnerships in AI research and development.

4. Empowering Individuals

AI Literacy

- Educating the public about AI is critical to fostering trust and reducing fear.

    - Example: Schools can include AI literacy programs that teach students how AI works and its ethical implications.

- Strategies for AI Literacy:

    - Develop free, accessible resources like online courses and community workshops.

    - Encourage media outlets to report on AI in a balanced and accurate way.

User Control

- People should have control over how AI systems interact with their lives.

    - Example: A user should be able to opt out of AI-driven personalization on social media platforms.

- Strategies for Empowerment:

    - Design AI systems with customizable settings.

    - Ensure users can review and delete their data from AI-driven platforms.

5. Involving Communities
Participatory Design

- Involve communities in the design and implementation of AI systems to ensure they meet local needs.

    - Example: A city council consults residents before deploying an AI-powered traffic management system.

- Strategies for Inclusion:

    - Host public forums where citizens can voice concerns and provide input.

    - Partner with community organizations to co-develop AI solutions.

Addressing Local Challenges

- Use AI to tackle region-specific issues, such as resource allocation or disaster management.

    - Example: An AI system helps a drought-prone region optimize water usage for agriculture.

6. The Role of Businesses
Ethical Business Practices

- Companies must prioritize long-term societal benefits over short-term profits.

  - Example: A tech company invests in creating AI tools for accessibility, such as real-time sign language translation.

- Strategies for Ethical Development:

  - Publish ethical guidelines and ensure all employees are trained in AI ethics.

  - Commit to open-source initiatives that allow public scrutiny of AI systems.

Building Customer Trust

- Businesses must demonstrate that their AI systems are safe, fair, and beneficial.

  - Example: A bank using AI for loan approvals ensures transparency by explaining the criteria used to evaluate applications.

- Strategies for Building Trust:

  - Use third-party audits to verify the fairness and accuracy of AI systems.

  - Offer customer support that addresses concerns about AI-driven decisions.

7. Encouraging Ethical Innovation

Incentivizing Responsible AI

- Governments and organizations can reward companies that prioritize ethical AI development.

- Example: Create awards or tax incentives for AI systems that address social challenges like healthcare access or environmental conservation.

Investing in Research

- Fund research into AI safety, fairness, and human-AI collaboration.

- Example: A nonprofit supports studies on how AI can be used to combat misinformation.

8. A Vision for a Trusted AI Future

Transparency by Default

- AI systems become open and understandable, earning trust through clarity and honesty.

Global Standards

- Nations align on ethical guidelines, ensuring that AI benefits humanity as a whole.

Empowered Users

- Individuals are equipped with the knowledge and tools to navigate AI systems confidently.

Chapter 27: AI and the Environment – A Tool for Sustainability

The Environmental Crisis
In a world grappling with climate change, deforestation, and dwindling resources, the challenges seem overwhelming. However, AI is emerging as a powerful tool to address these issues. By analyzing data, predicting outcomes, and optimizing systems, AI is helping humanity take meaningful steps toward a sustainable future.

This chapter explores how AI can be harnessed to protect the planet, highlighting both its potential and the challenges that come with its implementation.

1. AI in Climate Change Mitigation
Predicting Climate Patterns

- AI models analyze historical and real-time data to predict the impacts of climate change more accurately.

    - Example: AI-powered systems predict the frequency and intensity of hurricanes, allowing communities to prepare and adapt.

Optimizing Renewable Energy

- AI enhances the efficiency of renewable energy systems like solar, wind, and hydroelectric power.

    - Example: AI algorithms adjust wind turbine angles in real-time to maximize energy output based on weather conditions.

- Smart Grids: AI manages energy distribution, reducing waste and improving reliability.

Carbon Capture and Storage

- AI identifies optimal locations for carbon storage and monitors systems that capture and store CO_2.

2. Sustainable Agriculture

Precision Farming

- AI analyzes soil health, weather patterns, and crop needs to optimize planting, irrigation, and fertilization.

  - Example: AI-powered drones monitor crop health, identifying areas that require intervention.

Reducing Waste

- AI systems help farmers reduce waste by predicting harvest yields and optimizing supply chains.

  - Example: An AI platform connects farmers directly with consumers, reducing food spoilage during transportation.

Combatting Pests and Diseases

- AI tools detect early signs of crop diseases or pest infestations, preventing large-scale losses.

3. Protecting Biodiversity

Wildlife Monitoring

- AI-powered cameras and drones track animal populations and migration patterns, helping conservationists protect endangered species.

  - Example: AI systems analyze camera trap images to identify species and count individuals in real time.

Fighting Poaching

- AI monitors illegal activities in protected areas using surveillance systems and predictive analytics.

  - Example: AI detects unusual movement patterns in national parks, alerting authorities to potential poaching incidents.

Restoring Ecosystems

- AI helps design reforestation and habitat restoration projects by identifying the most effective strategies.

4. AI in Waste Management

Recycling Optimization

- AI-powered sorting systems identify and separate recyclable materials more efficiently than human workers.

  - Example: AI robots in recycling plants distinguish between plastics, metals, and paper, reducing contamination in recycling streams.

Reducing E-Waste

- AI helps design products with longer lifespans and easier repairability, reducing electronic waste.

  - Example: AI systems analyze product usage data to suggest designs that minimize resource consumption.

5. Urban Sustainability

Smart Cities

- AI systems optimize traffic flow, reduce energy consumption, and improve waste management in urban areas.

- Example: AI-powered traffic lights adapt to real-time conditions, reducing congestion and emissions.

Green Infrastructure

- AI identifies opportunities for urban greening, such as planting trees to reduce heat islands and improve air quality.

- Example: AI models suggest optimal locations for green roofs and urban parks.

Water Management

- AI predicts water demand, detects leaks, and optimizes distribution to reduce waste.

6. Challenges of Using AI for Sustainability

Energy Consumption

- While AI can promote sustainability, training and running AI models require significant energy.

- Example: Training a single large AI model can emit as much CO_2 as five cars over their lifetime.

Data Gaps

- Many regions lack the high-quality data needed for AI systems to be effective.

Equity and Access

- Developing countries may struggle to access AI tools for sustainability, exacerbating global inequalities.

Unintended Consequences

- Over-reliance on AI could lead to unforeseen environmental impacts, such as resource depletion in areas targeted for renewable energy projects.

7. Solutions for Ethical AI in Sustainability

Green AI Development

- Focus on energy-efficient algorithms and sustainable data centers to reduce AI's environmental footprint.

  - Example: Use renewable energy to power data centers that run AI systems.

Global Collaboration

- Share AI tools and resources with developing nations to ensure equitable access to sustainability solutions.

  - Example: An international initiative trains local experts in using AI for environmental monitoring.

Community Engagement

- Involve local communities in designing AI-driven sustainability projects to ensure they address real needs.

Transparency and Accountability

- Require organizations to publish environmental impact assessments for their AI projects.

8. Inspiring Examples of AI for Sustainability

IBM's Green Horizon Project

- Uses AI to analyze and reduce air pollution in cities by optimizing industrial operations and traffic flow.

Rainforest Connection

- Employs AI-powered sensors in forests to detect illegal logging and alert authorities.

Google's Environmental Insights Explorer

- Provides cities with data on building emissions and transportation patterns, helping them plan for a greener future.

AI is not a silver bullet for solving environmental challenges, but it is a powerful tool that, when used responsibly, can drive meaningful change.

- *The key lies in collaboration, innovation, and a commitment to sustainability, ensuring that AI contributes to a healthier, greener planet for future generations.*

"AI and Us: Navigating the Future of Work, Creativity, and Ethics"

Pioneering the Cosmos
On a distant planet, a rover equipped with AI navigates rocky terrain, analyzing soil samples for signs of life. Back on Earth, astronomers use AI to sift through terabytes of data, discovering new exoplanets in faraway galaxies. AI is transforming humanity's quest to explore the cosmos, breaking barriers that once seemed insurmountable.

This chapter delves into how AI is revolutionizing space exploration, from deep-space missions to understanding our place in the universe.

1. AI in Deep-Space Missions
Autonomous Rovers and Spacecraft

- AI enables spacecraft and rovers to operate independently, making decisions without waiting for instructions from Earth.

    - Example: NASA's Perseverance rover uses AI to navigate the Martian surface, avoiding obstacles and identifying areas of interest.

Mission Planning

- AI systems optimize flight paths, fuel usage, and mission timelines for efficiency and safety.

    - Example: AI algorithms planned the trajectory for the Parker Solar Probe, allowing it to fly closer to the Sun than any spacecraft before.

Surviving Harsh Environments

- AI helps space probes adapt to extreme conditions, such as radiation and temperature fluctuations.

  - Example: The Huygens probe used AI to analyze data as it descended through Titan's dense atmosphere.

2. AI and the Search for Extraterrestrial Life

Analyzing Planetary Data

- AI processes vast amounts of data collected by telescopes, rovers, and satellites to identify signs of life.

  - Example: AI systems analyze chemical compositions of exoplanet atmospheres to detect potential biosignatures, such as oxygen or methane.

Exploring Oceans Beyond Earth

- AI-powered submarines could explore the icy oceans of Europa or Enceladus, searching for microbial life.

SETI and AI

- The Search for Extraterrestrial Intelligence (SETI) uses AI to analyze radio signals for patterns that might indicate alien communication.

  - Example: AI algorithms sift through millions of signals daily, identifying those that deviate from natural patterns.

3. AI in Astronomical Discoveries

Mapping the Universe

- AI processes data from space telescopes to create detailed maps of galaxies, stars, and black holes.

- Example: The Gaia mission uses AI to map the Milky Way in unprecedented detail, identifying billions of stars.

Discovering Exoplanets

- AI analyzes light curves from distant stars to identify exoplanets passing in front of them.

  - Example: NASA's TESS mission discovered over 200 confirmed exoplanets with the help of AI.

Understanding Cosmic Phenomena

- AI models simulate the behavior of black holes, supernovae, and galaxy formation.

  - Example: AI helped scientists confirm the first detection of gravitational waves by analyzing data from LIGO.

4. AI and Space Sustainability

Managing Space Debris

- AI tracks space debris and predicts collisions, ensuring the safety of satellites and spacecraft.

  - Example: AI algorithms provide collision-avoidance recommendations for the International Space Station.

Optimizing Satellite Networks

- AI ensures efficient communication and energy use among satellite constellations, such as SpaceX's Starlink.

Sustainable Resource Utilization

- AI helps identify and manage resources on the Moon, Mars, and asteroids for future colonization efforts.

5. AI and Human Space Exploration
Supporting Astronauts

- AI assists astronauts by monitoring health, automating routine tasks, and providing real-time guidance.

  - Example: CIMON, an AI assistant aboard the ISS, helps astronauts with scientific experiments and technical troubleshooting.

Training for Space Missions

- AI-powered simulations prepare astronauts for complex scenarios, such as spacecraft malfunctions or planetary landings.

Future Colonies

- AI will play a crucial role in building and managing human colonies on other planets, optimizing life support systems, agriculture, and infrastructure.

6. Challenges of Using AI in Space
Data Transmission Delays

- Communication delays between Earth and deep-space missions make real-time decision-making difficult, requiring highly autonomous AI systems.

Energy Constraints

- AI systems on spacecraft must operate efficiently, as power supplies are limited.

Ethical Concerns

- As AI takes on more decision-making roles, questions arise about accountability and the prioritization of resources in space.

7. The Future of AI in Space Exploration

Interstellar Missions

- AI could enable humanity to explore beyond our solar system, operating spacecraft for decades or centuries.

    - Example: The Breakthrough Starshot initiative envisions AI-powered probes traveling to Alpha Centauri.

Terraforming and Resource Management

- AI could help terraform planets like Mars, analyzing environmental changes and optimizing resource usage.

Understanding the Universe

- AI might one day help answer fundamental questions about the nature of the universe, from dark matter to the origins of life.

8. Collaborative Efforts in AI and Space

Global Cooperation

- Space agencies, private companies, and research institutions must collaborate to develop AI systems for exploration.

    - Example: The European Space Agency and NASA collaborate on AI-driven projects to study Mars and beyond.

Private Sector Innovations

- Companies like SpaceX, Blue Origin, and Planet Labs are advancing AI technologies for commercial space travel and resource exploration.

- *AI is our partner in unlocking the mysteries of the universe, enabling us to go further than ever before.*

- *As we venture into the final frontier, we must ensure that our innovations reflect our highest values: curiosity, responsibility, and the pursuit of knowledge.*

Chapter 29: Humanity's Role in an AI-Driven World

The Intersection of Progress and Purpose

The world stands at the crossroads of unprecedented technological advancements and profound societal challenges. AI, a tool of incredible power, has the potential to redefine every aspect of life. But amid this transformation, one question looms large: *What is humanity's role in an AI-driven world?*

This final chapter reflects on the themes explored in this book and presents a vision for a future where AI serves as a partner, not a replacement, to humanity.

1. Embracing Our Strengths

The Uniqueness of Humanity

- While AI excels at processing data, it lacks qualities that define the human experience: empathy, creativity, and ethical reasoning.

- Example: A teacher not only imparts knowledge but also inspires and supports students in ways no machine can replicate.

Focusing on What Machines Can't Do

- Humanity's role lies in areas where AI cannot compete:

    - Building relationships.

    - Solving ethical dilemmas.

    - Pursuing creative and spiritual growth.

2. Shaping AI to Reflect Human Values

The Need for Ethical AI Development

- AI must be designed to reflect humanity's highest values, such as fairness, inclusivity, and responsibility.

  - Example: Developers prioritize transparency in AI systems to ensure they are accountable and trustworthy.

Human Oversight and Control

- Humans must remain at the center of decision-making processes, particularly in areas like healthcare, governance, and warfare.

  - Example: Doctors use AI to assist with diagnoses but retain ultimate responsibility for patient care.

3. Reimagining Success in an AI World

Beyond Productivity

- In an AI-driven world, success must be measured by more than economic output.

  - Example: Societies focus on well-being, sustainability, and social equity as key indicators of progress.

Balancing Technology and Humanity

- Embrace AI as a tool for enhancing human life while ensuring it does not dominate or replace meaningful human activities.

  - Example: Workers use AI to automate mundane tasks, freeing them to focus on creative and strategic projects.

4. Collaborating for a Better Future
Global Cooperation

- AI offers a unique opportunity for humanity to unite across borders to address shared challenges.

  - Example: Nations collaborate to use AI in combating climate change and eradicating diseases.

Public Involvement

- Ordinary citizens must play an active role in shaping AI policies and practices to ensure technology serves everyone.

  - Example: Community forums allow people to voice concerns and provide input on local AI initiatives.

5. The Vision for the Future
A Harmonious Partnership

- AI and humanity coexist in a partnership where each complements the other's strengths.

  - Example: AI tools enhance creativity, productivity, and efficiency, while humans focus on ethics, relationships, and innovation.

A World of Opportunities

- By leveraging AI responsibly, society can create opportunities for growth, discovery, and connection that were previously unimaginable.

Empowering Future Generations

- Preparing children for an AI-driven world ensures that they inherit a future where technology enhances, rather than diminishes, human potential.

6. A Call to Action

For Individuals

- Embrace lifelong learning to stay relevant and adaptable in a changing world.

- Advocate for responsible AI use in your community and workplace.

- Focus on building connections, creativity, and empathy—qualities that machines cannot replicate.

For Governments and Organizations

- Invest in education, infrastructure, and policies that prepare society for AI's impact.

- Ensure AI development prioritizes ethical considerations and equitable access.

- Foster global collaboration to address challenges that no single nation can solve alone.

7. Closing Reflection

The chapter ends with a hopeful vision:

- *AI is not the end of humanity—it is a new beginning. By embracing this technology with wisdom, compassion, and purpose, we can shape a future that reflects the best of who we are.*

The final paragraph challenges readers to take an active role in shaping the future:

- *The decisions we make today will determine the world we create tomorrow. Together, we can ensure that AI becomes a tool for progress, not a source of division; a partner, not a threat. The future is in our hands.*

Looking Ahead

The epilogue reflects on the themes of the book and reiterates its central message: AI is a tool, and its ultimate impact depends on how humanity chooses to use it. By embracing our unique strengths, collaborating globally, and prioritizing ethical development, we can create a future where technology serves humanity, not the other way around.

A Future Worth Building

As we stand on the precipice of a new era defined by artificial intelligence, we must remember one simple truth: technology is a reflection of the values and intentions of those who create it. AI holds immense potential to amplify human capabilities, solve global challenges, and reshape our lives in ways we cannot yet fully comprehend. But it is not an autonomous force—it is a tool, and its impact will depend on the wisdom, responsibility, and humanity we bring to its development and use.

This book has explored both the opportunities and challenges of AI, highlighting its role in transforming industries, redefining creativity, and reshaping what it means to work, learn, and live. It has also emphasized the importance of ethics, collaboration, and balance in ensuring that AI serves as a partner in building a future that reflects our highest ideals.

To those reading these final words, I leave you with a challenge: take an active role in shaping this future. Whether as an educator, policymaker, developer, artist, parent, or curious individual, your actions matter. Advocate for fairness, support innovation, prioritize sustainability, and ensure that technology serves humanity—not the other way around.

The story of AI is not yet written. Its chapters will be crafted by the collective efforts of people around the world, guided by a shared vision of a better, more equitable future. Together, we can ensure that AI becomes a tool for progress, a beacon of hope, and a testament to what humanity can achieve when it leads with purpose and compassion.

The future isn't something that happens to us—it's something we build. Let's build it well.

Acknowledgments: A Heartfelt Thank You

Writing this book has been an incredible journey, one filled with curiosity, discovery, and reflection. It would not have been possible without the contributions, support, and inspiration of many people who have helped shape its vision and message.

To my readers: Thank you for investing your time and energy in this exploration of AI and its future. Your curiosity, critical thinking, and desire to engage with this subject matter are what give this work its meaning. It is my hope that this book has inspired you to ask questions, imagine possibilities, and take action in shaping the future.

To the innovators and visionaries who are advancing the field of AI responsibly: Your dedication to creating technologies that serve humanity is a testament to the power of human ingenuity. Thank you for paving the way for a brighter future.

To the teachers, parents, and leaders who guide the next generation: Your work is vital in preparing society for the opportunities and challenges of an AI-driven world. Thank you for inspiring hope, fostering resilience, and nurturing the potential of those who will inherit the future.

To my support system: Whether directly or indirectly, your encouragement has been a source of strength. Your belief in the importance of this project has kept me motivated and grounded.

Finally, to the collective human spirit: Our ability to dream, create, and collaborate is what makes progress possible. AI may transform the tools we use, but it is our shared humanity that will always guide us toward a better tomorrow.

This book is a reflection of collective wisdom and shared purpose. I am deeply grateful to everyone who has contributed, inspired, or simply supported its creation. Together, we are shaping the future—thank you for being part of it.

With gratitude,

Alan MOUHLI

Key Takeaways

- AI is a tool that reflects human values; its impact depends on how we choose to develop and use it.

- Humanity's role lies in areas where machines cannot compete—empathy, creativity, ethical reasoning, and adaptability.

- Education, collaboration, and ethical frameworks are essential to prepare society for the challenges and opportunities of an AI-driven world.